IMAGES
of America

CONNECTICUT MINING

IMAGES
of America

CONNECTICUT MINING

John A. Pawloski

ARCADIA
PUBLISHING

Published by Arcadia Publishing
Charleston, South Carolina

Library of Congress Catalog Card Number: 2006923203

For all general information contact Arcadia Publishing at:
Telephone 843-853-2070
Fax 843-853-0044
E-mail sales@arcadiapublishing.com
For customer service and orders:
Toll-Free 1-888-313-2665

Visit us on the Internet at www.arcadiapublishing.com

To Charles Rufus Harte (1870–1956), a civil engineer and historian
who had the wisdom to preserve much of Connecticut's history on
30,000 film negatives. The printing of over 2,000 mining related
negatives from his collection inspired the writing of this book,
and Harte's photographs form the core of this publication.

CONTENTS

ACKNOWLEDGMENTS

I wish to thank Frederick W. Chesson, who graciously loaned me the Harte collection of negatives; Charles Rufus Harte Jr., for permission to use his father's photographs; and to the many individuals, museums, historical societies, libraries, and mining companies who opened their archives for my use. I also wish to thank Dawn Robertson of Arcadia Publishing for support and criticism and my wife, Patricia, for her patience, understanding, and tolerance of my work. My sincerest thanks to Kathy DelMonico and my son, John A. Pawloski Jr., for their many hours devoted to editing this manuscript.

INTRODUCTION

The search for mineral wealth in Connecticut has spanned over 10,000 years. It began with the migration of Native Americans into the Northeast soon after the last of the glaciers had melted away.

The Native Americans used many natural materials in their daily lives including stones, which gave the best cutting edges and were consequently used as tools. Stones came from streams, beach, or glacial gravel. Also, deposits of basalt, steatite, and quartz were intentionally sought after and mined by the Native Americans.

European colonists who arrived in North America in the early 1600s began a change that would have a profound impact on this continent and on all corners of the earth. It was the intent of these early explorers to search out and claim deposits of gold, silver, and precious gems. However, it was soon realized that these deposits of precious gems and metals were few and of low quality.

These early prospectors did, however, pave the way for the colonists who initiated the search for less valuable, but more utilitarian metals such as iron, copper, and lead. These metals were essential to colonists to establishing civilization as they knew it in a strange and hostile land.

The survival of the earliest colonists was precarious. Communication with the mother country was unpredictable and supplies came slowly. Colonists had to use familiar materials and tools, and nails, axes, hammers, and cooking utensils were among their most precious belongings. Many of these items were made from iron and it is not surprising that North America's first mining and smelting operation in the colonies was to produce this metal.

Although blacksmiths made small amounts of iron from ore in their forges, the onerous title of the "First Iron Maker" goes to John Winthrop Jr., who established the first working iron furnace in North America in Braintree, Massachusetts, in 1644. Soon after, Winthrop established another more successful iron furnace in Saugus, Massachusetts.

Winthrop's father encouraged him to move to the Connecticut Colony, and John Winthrop Jr. soon was chosen governor, and while in that position he encouraged the exploration for natural resources and paved the way for Connecticut's significant mining heritage.

In 1651, Winthrop directed the construction and operation of the fourth iron furnace in North America, near Lake Saltonstall in North Branford. The Branford furnace remained in operation until 1680.

Since Connecticut provided many of the "firsts" in the history of North American mining, it has been christened the "cradle of American mining." The first copper mine began in Simsbury, now East Granby, in 1705 and is presently the site of Old Newgate Prison State Historical Park.

Mining in the country's first sandstone quarry began in Hartford in 1639. The nation's first granite quarry was located on land owned by John Winthrop Jr. at Millstone Point, Waterford, in 1648. Barite was first mined in the United States in Cheshire, which remained the primary producer of this ore for many years. Other firsts include the mines for tungsten, bismuth, cobalt, and nickel. The nation's first feldspar grinding mill was located in Glastonbury. Eli Whitney Blake, of New Haven, invented the mechanical rock crusher in 1858, which gave birth to the crushed stone industry.

During the Revolutionary War, Connecticut was considered the "arsenal of the Revolution" because of the large numbers of cannons and cannonballs produced from the iron furnace in Salisbury. Without production of military materials from these furnaces it is possible that the war for independence from England might not have succeeded.

Mining in Connecticut reached its peak sometime in the second half of the 19th century as the ores became depleted. This coincided with the discovery of larger, richer deposits of ore in the western states.

Today, there are no metal mines in Connecticut. Connecticut's largest mining industry is aggregate (crushed stone), used in the manufacturing of concrete and for paving. Minor amounts of granite, brownstone, and clay are also being mined.

One

IRON THAT HELPED BUILD A NATION

An ore is any mineral that can be mined and smelted in a commercially economic way. The earliest iron furnaces in New England utilized bog ore, which consists of iron oxides scraped from the bottom of swamps and ponds. Bog ore is not very plentiful, but it worked well for its time period, and Winthrop's furnace in North Branford used bog ore.

In 1730, a major deposit of brown hematite iron ore was discovered in frontier northwestern Connecticut, in what was to become the town of Salisbury. The ore was rich and plentiful, and kept the blast furnaces in operation until 1923.

The Ore Hill Mine in Salisbury was the largest producer of iron ore in Connecticut. It began as a series of small, independently owned open pits that were eventually consolidated into one large mine. The average annual yield of the mines between 1796 and 1835 was about 5,000 tons of ore per year. Underground mining commenced at a depth of 100 feet, and the inclined tunnels extended eastward for over two miles and reached a depth of about 430 feet. There were many lateral tunnels, called drifts, where the ore was mined. Pillars 30 feet square were left between the drifts to keep the ground stable.

Iron furnaces required a reliable source of water to power the air blast machinery, and were located a number of miles from the mines. The ore was transported from the mine to the furnace in ox-drawn wagons, and subsequently by railroad.

In the early 1900s, the Ore Hill Mine employed about 200 men and children. These children, between the ages of 10 and 14, were hired to load the ore into wagons, and endured a work day that was 12 hours long.

There were numerous other similar iron deposits in the area, also in neighboring New York and Massachusetts. This region termed the Salisbury Iron District was world famous for the quality of iron cast from the districts furnaces.

This map from the 1874 *Beer's Atlas of Litchfield County, Connecticut*, shows the location of three iron companies, which mined the Ore Hill deposit in the town of Salisbury. The Brook Pit Mining Company established a company town with housing, school, and a company store for their employees. The "Iron Ore Bed" shows the location of the mine. (*Beer's Atlas of Litchfield County, Connecticut*, 1874, John A. Pawloski collection.)

This photograph displays an inclined hoist at the Ore Hill Mine. Initially ox-drawn carts were used to haul the ore from the bottom of the pit, and then later, a steam powered inclined skip car was used to haul the ore to the surface where the ore was washed and sorted prior to shipping to the furnace. The low grade ore and waste rock was put into piles called dumps. (Courtesy of Frederick Chesson, photograph by Charles R. Harte.)

10

In 1885, when the Ore Hill pit reached the depth of about 100 feet, underground mining commenced. This photograph, taken around 1900, shows Ore Hill laborers loading a mine car with ore. In the background, one can see log timbers used for supporting the roof of the tunnel. Although blasting was used to break up rock at this mine, much of the ore was friable enough so that most of the ore was removed using only a pick. (Courtesy of the Salisbury Association.)

An ore skip is a rail mounted car used for hoisting rock along an inclined track. When the car reaches the top of the hoist, the rock is dumped out, and the car returned to the bottom of the shaft, or in this case, the pit. This particular skip was used at the Ore Hill Mine. (Courtesy of Frederick Chesson, photograph by Charles R. Harte.)

Once the rock is hoisted by the skip to the surface it is dumped into one of two piles: waste or ore. The ore is then washed and sorted by size and quality. The waste, called gangue, is carted to the dump pile and the ore loaded into oxcarts or rail cars for transporting to the blast furnace. This photograph is of the washing area of the Ore Hill Mine in Salisbury. (Courtesy of W. H. C. Pychon, *Connecticut Magazine*, 1899.)

This 1870s stereopticon photograph shows a series of mule-drawn carts hauling ore out of the Ore Hill Mine in Salisbury. Each cart was pulled by a team of mules up a series of switchbacks in order to reach the surface of the mine. (Courtesy of Frederic Chesson, Charles R. Harte collection.)

A stereopticon photograph, taken in the 1870s, shows a mule skinner preparing to dump a cart load of waste rock into the mine dump area of the Ore Hill Mine, Salisbury. As seen in this photograph, there is a tremendous quantity of gangue removed during a mining operation. (Courtesy of Frederick Chesson, Charles R. Harte collection.)

With the possibility of the United States entering World War II, the government requested that the Salisbury Iron District mines be examined to see if it would be feasible to reopen them for the war effort, but none of the mines were reopened. This photograph, taken November 27, 1941, is of James Flint who was part of the evaluation team at Ore Hill in Salisbury. (Courtesy of Frederick Chesson, photograph by Charles R. Harte.)

This is an early-1900s photograph of the Davis Mine located in Lakeville. Like most of the Salisbury district mines, the Davis Mine (also called the Henderson Mine) was an open pit operation. The Davis Mine was first worked in 1734, and the construction of the hoisting works can be seen in the lower left portion of the photograph. (Courtesy of Frederick Chesson, Charles R. Harte collection.)

The South Kent ore bed consisted of three mines in the vicinity of Hatch Pond. The earliest attempt to work this deposit as an open pit operation began in 1733. In 1854, the mines were purchased by the Kent Iron Company, who sank shafts to a depth of 300 feet into the ore. This 1935 photograph shows the ruins of the mine office building. (Courtesy of Frederick Chesson, photograph by Charles R. Harte.)

The Mine Hill iron mine is located in Roxbury. Mine Hill is unique because the ore is primarily siderite (iron carbonate), all mining was underground, and the furnace was only one half mile away. Mine Hill was first worked in 1753 for silver, which was found intermixed with the iron ore. This photograph taken in 1934 is of the main (lowermost) tunnel. (Courtesy of Frederick Chesson, photograph by Charles R. Harte.)

15

The entrance to the Mine Hill tunnel is supported by cement arches constructed by the students from the Columbia Mining College (now Columbia University) in the early 1900s. These supports were made outside the tunnel and hoisted in place by the students. This view is from inside the mine, looking out. (Courtesy of Frederick Chesson, photograph by Charles R. Harte.)

The mining of iron at Mine Hill began in earnest in 1864. As the miners removed the ore, it was necessary for them to support certain weak areas of the mine with timbers, or even concrete in some places. This 1965 photograph shows some of the timber supports in the lower tunnel. (Photograph by John A. Pawloski.)

In order to make iron, the ore needs to be smelted in a blast furnace. The ruins of the Mount Riga furnace, one of the earliest in Connecticut, can be seen in this 1933 photograph. The Mount Riga furnace went into blast around 1781 and was shut down in 1856. (Courtesy of Frederick Chesson, photograph by Charles R. Harte.)

The Mount Riga furnace produced all the iron used in the building of the U.S.S. *Constitution*, as well as much of the iron used by the Springfield and Harper's Ferry arsenals for making guns. The furnace structure was restored in the late 1930s. (Courtesy of Frederick Chesson, Charles R. Harte collection.)

There were three iron furnaces along the Blackberry River in East Canaan. This photograph, taken around 1875, is of the No. 3 furnace built and operated by the Barnum-Richardson Company in 1872. The No. 3 furnace remained in operation until 1923 and was the last blast furnace in operation in Connecticut. In front of the building are stacks of pig iron. (Courtesy of Frederick Chesson, Charles R. Harte collection.)

The No. 1 furnace, or Forbes furnace, was built in 1832 along the Blackberry River, and remained in operation until 1880. Iron furnaces were constructed along rivers in order to harness the water to power bellows and/or blowing engines that produced the air blast. The Barnum-Richardson Company purchased the Forbes furnace in 1862. This photograph was taken around 1875. (Courtesy of Frederick Chesson, Charles R. Harte collection.)

The Canaan No. 2 furnace, or Beckley furnace, was built in 1846 along the Blackberry River. The stone furnace can be seen near the center of the picture the top of which is enclosed by the charging bridge. This photograph was taken around 1875, prior to its modernization by the Barnum-Richardson Company in 1880. The No. 2 furnace went out of blast in 1919. (Courtesy of Frederick Chesson, Charles R. Harte collection.)

The buildings in the upper left are charcoal storage sheds. The multi-window building in this photograph shows the Canaan No. 2 (Beckley furnace) and charging bridge after they were modernized. The charging bridge is where the ore, charcoal, and flux are dumped into the top of the furnace for smelting. The furnace is barely visible behind the curved roof of the casting shed. (Courtesy of Frederick Chesson, Charles R. Harte collection.)

The Chapinville furnace, located in Salisbury, began operation in 1826. Early iron furnaces were of the cold blast type, which means that the air blast was not preheated before entering the furnace. In 1856, the Chapinville furnace was converted to a hot blast. This photograph shows the dismantling of the furnace building sometime after operations ceased in 1897. (Courtesy of Frederick Chesson, Charles R. Harte collection.)

The Hunts-Lyman Iron Company (Huntsville furnace), was located in Huntsville, just east of Falls Village. The furnace consisted of a single stack with an open top. The iron produced from this furnace was used in the manufacture of railroad car wheels. The Huntsville furnace was purchased by the Barnum-Richardson Company around 1872. This photograph was taken around 1875. (Courtesy of Frederick Chesson, Charles R. Harte collection.)

Like almost all Connecticut iron furnaces, time takes its toll on the structures and can be seen in this photograph of the Huntsville furnace taken in 1935, showing only the stack remaining. One unusual feature of this furnace is the rounded arch compared to the typical Gothic arch used in most furnaces. (Courtesy of Frederick Chesson, photograph by Charles R. Harte.)

As the Huntsville furnace collapsed, the internal structure was revealed. The core of the furnace, called the bosh, is made of several layers of refractory brick. The two pipes for heating the air blast can be seen along side the bosh. Next to the bosh is a layer of sand, then small rocks, and finally the stone masonry exterior. (Courtesy of Frederick Chesson, photograph by Charles R. Harte.)

The Cornwall Bridge iron furnace was built in 1833 along Furnace Brook. Initially it utilized a cold air blast and then was converted to hot blast around 1866 after its purchase by the Barnum-Richardson Company. This photograph, taken around 1875, reveals the use of a covered flume supplying the water for the wheel-powered blowing tubs (lower part of the photograph). The furnace was closed in 1897. (Courtesy of Frederick Chesson, Charles R. Harte collection.)

The Lime Rock furnace was built in 1825, and in 1863 was purchased by the Barnum-Richardson Company and then rebuilt. The Lime Rock furnace and foundry was world famous for making cast rolls for rolling mills and for chilled railroad car wheels. The furnace closed in 1900. This photograph was taken around 1875. (Courtesy of Frederick Chesson, Charles R. Harte collection.)

This postcard view, taken around 1890 of the Lime Rock furnace, shows the charcoal sheds on the left and the casting shed in the lower right. The furnace is located behind the casting shed, and has smoke coming from the chimney. (Courtesy of John A. Pawloski.)

If a particular product has to be cast, such as a railroad car wheel, the molten iron has to be transferred from the furnace to the mold. The wheeled ladle seen in this photograph was used for this purpose at Lime Rock. (Courtesy of Frederick Chesson, photograph by Charles R. Harte.)

This photograph, taken around 1875, is of the Barnum-Richardson Company office located in Lime Rock. By 1883, the Barnum-Richardson Company controlled eight of the nine iron furnaces in the Salisbury district, the exception being the Kent Iron Company. (Courtesy of Frederick Chesson, Charles R. Harte collection.)

The Barnum-Richardson foundry buildings are shown in this photograph. A large inventory of finished railroad car wheels can be seen in front of the nearest building in this c. 1875 photograph. (Courtesy of Frederick Chesson, Charles R. Harte collection.)

The Sharon Valley Iron Company, located in the town of Sharon, went into blast in 1825 and closed in 1898, after 73 years of operation. The ore for this furnace came from the Indian Lake ore bed and from Ore Hill. The Sharon Valley furnace was also purchased by the Barnum-Richardson Company in 1873. This photograph was taken around 1875. (Courtesy of Frederick Chesson, Charles R. Harte collection.)

The collapse of the stone masonry stack shows a well defined refractory brick-lined bosh of the Bulls Bridge furnace located just south of the covered bridge in Kent. The Bulls Bridge furnace began operation in 1826 and closed in 1865. (Courtesy of John A. Pawloski.)

The location of the Bulls Bridge furnace on a very picturesque section of the Housatonic River made it a very popular area to visit and it still is today. This *c.* 1895 photograph was taken by Clarence Evans. (Courtesy of John A. Pawloski.)

CAMP & FENN,

MANUFACTURERS OF

PIG IRON,

AT BULLS BRIDGE,

Town of Kent, Litchfield Co., Ct.

THEY MANUFACTURE A

SUPERIOR IRON

FOR

FOUNDERY & MACHINE PURPOSES.

The qualities of the Iron are,

IT RUNS CLOSE AND SMOOTH,

Is fine, grained soft Iron with strength combined, and is susceptible of a polish.

THERE IS A SAVING OF AT LEAST

Five per cent. in re-melting,

And it has been pronounced the

BEST AMERICAN IRON MADE.

The Kent town records show an ironworks at Bull's Falls as early as 1766. Later that year, Bull sold the operation to William Johnson and David Lewis. The Ousatonic Ironworks constructed the first furnace on the property in 1826; in 1851 Silas Camp and William Fenn purchased the property. This advertisement is from an 1851 Connecticut business directory. Several other companies operated the furnace until it closed. (Courtesy of Frederick Chesson, Charles R. Harte collection.)

STUART, HOPSON & CO.,

MANUFACTURERS OF

SALISBURY

PIG IRON,

KENT, CONN.

The Kent Iron Company had its origins as the Sand Plain furnace in 1825, was later operated by Stuart, Hopson and Company, and eventually by the Kent Iron Company. This advertisement from an 1851 Connecticut business directory claims production of "Salisbury pig iron," which is made from the brown hematite ore typically found in northwestern Connecticut. (Courtesy of Frederick Chesson, Charles R. Harte collection.)

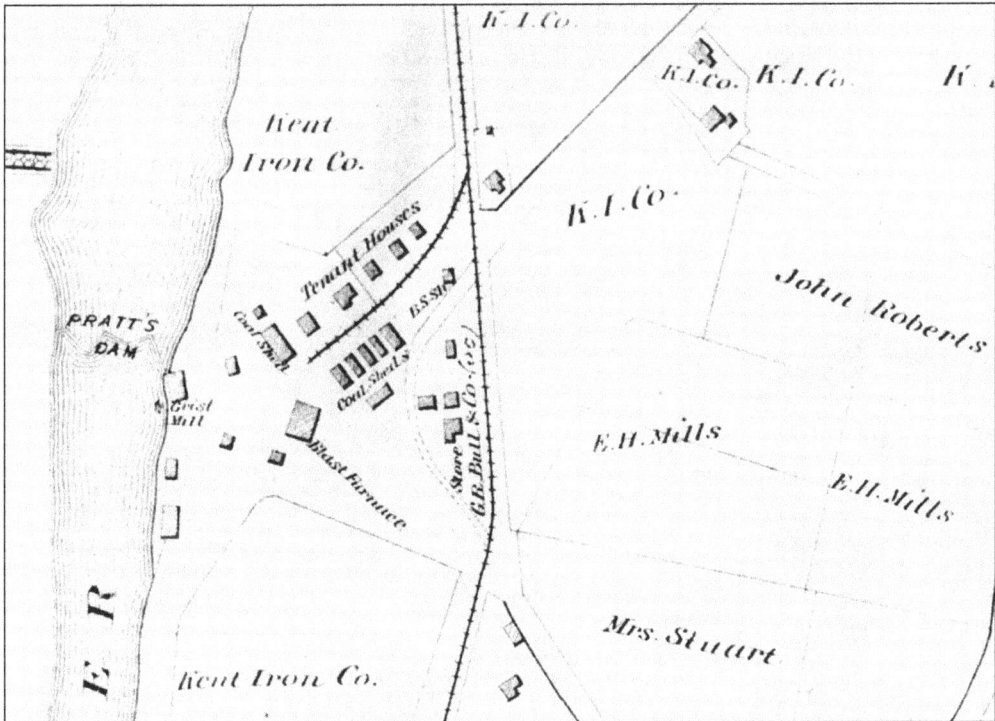

The 1874 *Beer's Atlas of Litchfield County, Connecticut*, contains a detailed map of the Kent Iron Company furnace complex, which besides the furnace and charcoal sheds consisted of a gristmill, blacksmith shop, company store, and houses for the workers. The Housatonic Railroad began operations in 1841. (Courtesy of John A. Pawloski.)

The Kent Iron Company closed in 1892 after a fire destroyed a large charcoal shed. This was the straw that broke the company's back, because the Connecticut iron industry was on the decline due to increased operating expenses and did not permit them to compete economically with the newer furnaces and vast ore and fuel deposits of the Midwest. The furnace is on the far left. (Courtesy of Frederick Chesson, Charles R. Harte collection.)

This view of the Kent Iron Company furnace was taken shortly after the furnace closed in 1892. Since iron furnaces were continuously loaded from the top of the stack, it was necessary for them to be built into a bank so the charging bridge would be level with the supply of raw materials. The charging bridge was covered to protect the fuel from moisture. (Courtesy of Frederick Chesson, Charles R. Harte collection.)

Pratt's dam across the Housatonic River was constructed of wood cribbing filled with stone. The water was diverted into a millrace to power a gristmill, the furnace blowing engines, and finally a sawmill before being returned to the river. This photograph, taken in 1935, shows the remains of the dam. (Courtesy of Frederick Chesson, photograph by Charles R. Harte.)

This photograph shows the waterwheel that powered the blowing engines for the iron furnace. Since the majority of all of the Connecticut iron furnaces depended upon water to power the blowing engines, a dependable supply was necessary. Furnaces were shut down in times of severe drought or during heavy freezes. (Courtesy of Frederick Chesson, photograph by Charles R. Harte.)

Blowing engines were developed to provide a larger, and more reliable, volume of air to the furnace. If the air source diminished, the temperature in the furnace would drop, the melt would freeze, and the furnace shut down. Blowing engines consisted of a pair of cylinders having alternating strokes of pistons, and an equalizer box to give a steady blast of air. (Courtesy of Frederick Chesson, photograph by Charles R. Harte.)

This photograph shows the interior of the charging bridge of the Kent furnace looking toward the charging arch where the raw materials were dumped into the furnace. The charge of raw materials consisted of ore, charcoal, and marble flux. A flux was used to aid in the smelting of ore and to remove impurities. The solidified glassy impurity, or waste, is called slag. (Courtesy of Frederick Chesson, Charles R. Harte collection.)

This 1874 map nicely shows the relationship between the mine and the iron smelting complex at Mine Hill in Roxbury. What is unique to this operation is that the mine is only one half mile from the furnace area. The mine was connected to the furnace by rail. Mules were used for braking, more than pulling, on the down hill run to the furnace. (*Beer's Atlas of Litchfield County, Connecticut,* 1874, John A. Pawloski collection.)

On one of Charles R. Harte's excursions to Mine Hill, he discovered a Blake rock crusher. The crusher was used to break the ore into smaller sizes. It should be noted that Eli Whitney Blake of New Haven invented the first mechanical rock crusher in 1858. Blake's invention created the crushed stone industry. (Courtesy of Frederick Chesson, photograph by Charles R. Harte.)

The iron ore, siderite, at Mine Hill contains a substantial quantity of sulfide minerals. This created a serious problem for the ironmaster if the ore was to be smelted into iron directly. The release of sulfurous gases could cause explosions within the furnace. This problem was rectified by roasting the ore prior to smelting. This 1934 photograph shows the double roasting furnace at Mine Hill. (Courtesy of Frederick Chesson, photograph by Charles R. Harte.)

The Mine Hill smelting furnace is made of beautifully crafted granite gneiss quarried on the property. The charging arch, where the raw materials are dumped into the furnace, is at the bottom of the brick chimney, the charging bridge is left of the chimney, and the casting shed is on the right of the furnace. (Courtesy of the Gunn Museum, photograph by Joseph West.)

In 1866, the Shepaug Spathic Iron and Steel Company, who developed the Mine Hill property, reorganized into the American Silver Steel Company. The furnace continued to be fraught with problems, and on May 10, 1872, it reorganized into the Shepaug Iron Company. The reorganization did nothing to improve conditions, so eight days later the furnace fires were extinguished forever. This illustration is a vignette from a stock certificate. (Courtesy of Frederick Chesson, Charles R. Harte collection.)

As early as 1820, the Barnum and Richardson families formed a partnership to operate a store in Lime Rock. Soon after, the partnership moved into the iron business, and by 1858, the partnership began to buy up the iron furnaces in northwestern Connecticut. The Barnum-Richardson Company specialized in products for the railroad industry, especially car wheels. This image is a late 1800s advertisement. (Courtesy of John A. Pawloski.)

This invoice, dated August 12, 1872, from the Barnum-Richardson Company to the Housatonic Railroad, is for 511 thirty-three-inch car wheels. The Barnum-Richardson Company shipped railroad products throughout the world. (Courtesy of John A. Pawloski.)

This advertising display of the Barnum-Richardson Company shows the furnaces, foundry, and office of the corporation. By 1883, the Barnum-Richardson Company controlled eight of the nine operating furnaces in northwestern Connecticut. By the early 1890s, the Salisbury iron industry began to fail, and one by one the Barnum-Richardson Company began to shut down their furnaces, the last being Canaan No. 3 in 1923. (Courtesy of Frederick Chesson, Charles R. Harte collection.)

No. 1 Lime Rock Furnace
" 2 Huntsville "
" 3 Sharon "
" 4 Millerton "
" 5 Foundries-Lime Rock

No. 6 Cornwall Bridge Furnace.
" 7 Canaan No. 1 "
8 " " 2 "
9 " " 3 "
" 10 Office-Lime Rock.

BARNUM RICHARDSON COMPANY'S
IRON WORKS.
SALISBURY, CONNECTICUT, U. S. A.

During the Civil War, the Ames Ironworks in Falls Village manufactured large artillery pieces for the Union Army. Horatio Ames, in the top hat, is standing next to an example of one of these. (Courtesy of Frederick Chesson, Charles R. Harte collection.)

Two

CHARCOAL TO FUEL THE FURNACES

Charcoal was the preferred fuel for the Connecticut iron furnaces for several reasons; it was easily made from the trees in the immediate area, it was abundant, it produced a high furnace temperature, and it made an excellent iron from Salisbury ore.

Charcoal is made by burning wood in a closed environment in order to drive off the volatile gasses and leave behind a relatively pure form of carbon. The production of charcoal for the iron furnaces was a year-round job for a trained group of men called colliers. During the winter months, small trees were cut into four foot lengths, and then stacked to dry. These short pieces of wood were called billets.

Charcoal burning took place during the warmer months. The collier chose a level area of ground for the pit, also called a heap or a milar, and the leaves were then raked away to form a circle about 20 feet in diameter. It took between 30 and 50 cords of wood to make a heap. The entire structure was then covered with a thick layer of leaves, and then a layer of dirt. Holes were punched at intervals around the heap to provide air for the wood to burn.

The heap was set on fire in the center where a sapling was placed. It was important to control the fire. This was done by controlling the amount of air that got to the fire. If the heap began to burn out of control the openings in the leaf-dirt layers had to be plugged. This sometimes required the collier to climb onto the top of the heap.

When the heap was a glowing mass of orange burning wood all the vents were plugged to extinguish the fire, and then the heap was allowed to cool for a number of days. The entire process of burning and cooling took about 12 days.

A typical Connecticut iron furnace used about 1,200 bushels of charcoal per day. By the mid-1800s, the hills of northwestern Connecticut were denuded of trees. Because of this local "fuel crisis," the iron companies purchased forest lands in New York, New Hampshire, and Vermont for charcoal production.

This photograph, taken in 1905 on Cream Hill, Cornwall, shows a woodchopper cutting billets of wood for making charcoal. Notice how few trees were left to reseed the area. In 1850, two men cut 250 cords of wood in that year for the production of charcoal. (Courtesy of the Cornwall Historical Society.)

A 1905 winter photograph of a portion of Cream Hill, Cornwall, shows a large area that has been cut for charcoal. What appear to be dots on the hill side are actually stacks of wood. The trees that remain on the ridge of the hill are mostly white pine, a wood that is unsuitable for charcoal. (Courtesy of the Cornwall Historical Society.)

This collier is stacking billets of slab wood in preparation for making charcoal. Slabs are the rounded outside part of a log that are removed when sawing the log into lumber. When the stacking is completed, the heap will be covered with a layer of leaves and a layer of dirt and then set on fire. (Courtesy of the New Milford Historical Society.)

COAL PIT

The terms coal pit, milar, and charcoal heap are essentially the same thing. When a charcoal heap is burned the heap shrinks in size. It is important for the collier to seal any breaks in the soil covering the heap that would cause it to burn to ashes. The small amounts of smoke can be seen coming from the air vents. (Courtesy of John A. Pawloski, photograph by Clarence Evans.)

This c. 1890 photograph shows a collier carrying a bushel of charcoal to his wagon. The bushel was the standard unit of measure for charcoal. The wagon was designed so that the floor boards could be easily pulled out to drop the load of charcoal. (Courtesy of the Falls Village-Canaan Historical Society.)

The burning process is a 12- to 15-day, 24-hour-per-day operation. The Colliers lived on site in small tipi-like huts made of logs covered with topsoil. Between "burns," the colliers would spend time with their families, as can be seen in this 1905 photograph taken at Cream Hill, Cornwall. (Courtesy of the Cornwall Historical Society.)

Three

THE MINOR METALS AND MINERALS

Connecticut is blessed with a tremendous variety of minerals. However, only a few have proven to be economical for mining. Iron was the most abundant and the most important metal resource mined in Connecticut and copper was second.

Connecticut has the honor of hosting the first colonial copper mining and smelting operation in North America. In 1707, the Newgate Mine deposit in East Granby was discovered. The Newgate Mine, also called the Simsbury Mine, was first worked under a charter granted by the Connecticut colonial government.

Between 1773 and 1831, the mine was used as a prison. The name Newgate was selected in honor of the infamous British prison. After the prison was closed, mining resumed on and off until 1901.

Not far from Newgate, Dr. Samuel Higley began mining copper in 1728. Since coinage was scarce in the colonies, Higley smelted some of the ore and minted coins of his own design. These Higley Coppers, the name given by numismatists, were the first copper coins minted in the colonies.

The richest copper deposit in Connecticut was in Bristol. The Bristol copper deposit, discovered in 1790, did not see serious mining commence until 1837. The mine was heavily worked between 1847 and 1854, and produced nearly $200,000 worth of copper in those seven years.

When the Bristol Copper Mine closed in 1895, the mine shafts had reached a depth of 600 feet, and there were hundreds of feet of drifts.

Lead was mined at several Connecticut locations. The largest and most active of these mines was in Middletown. During the Revolutionary War, lead was a strategic metal. Initially the mine was operated by British loyalists; however, a group of Connecticut Patriots quickly took over the mine, and subsequently several tons of lead shot for the colonial militia came from this mine.

The occurrence of tungsten minerals in the town of Trumbull was first unearthed in 1818. Until Thomas Edison perfected his light bulb using tungsten as the filament, there was virtually no use for the metal. Tungsten mining began here in 1897, and was the first in North America. But problems of removing impurities from the ore forced the closing of the mine in 1916.

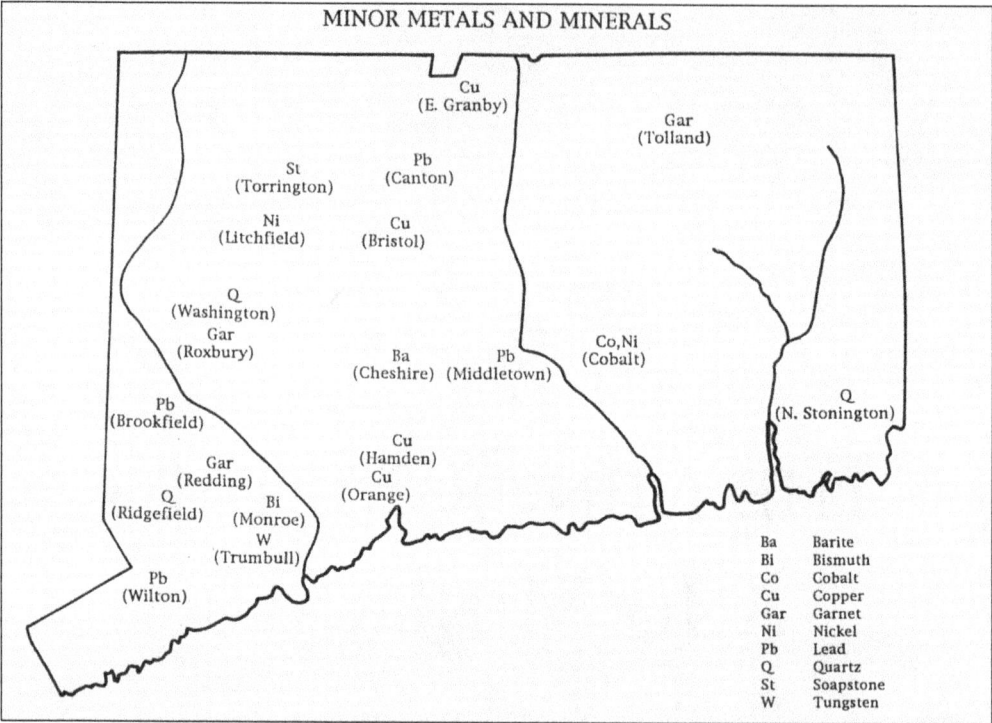

Ba	Barite
Bi	Bismuth
Co	Cobalt
Cu	Copper
Gar	Garnet
Ni	Nickel
Pb	Lead
Q	Quartz
St	Soapstone
W	Tungsten

There are well over 200 mines, quarries, and prospects in Connecticut. This map shows the generalized locations for some of the historically more important mines for the minor metals and minerals. (Created by John A. Pawloski.)

South View showing Guard Tower, Newgate Prison, East Granby, Conn.

This 1903 postcard shows a view of Old Newgate Prison in East Granby, site of the first colonial copper mine in North America. Mining at Newgate began in 1707, and just over 100 tons of ore was mined and shipped to Great Britain for smelting. In 1773, the mine was converted into a prison, and the prisoners were forced to work in the mine. (Courtesy of John A. Pawloski.)

42

This 1903 postcard photograph of the Newgate Copper Mine in East Granby shows the bottom of the 80 foot shaft and the entrance to the drain where a prisoner made his escape. Hundreds of feet of tunnels were dug in pursuit of copper ore. Today the prison and tunnels are preserved as a State Historic Park. (Courtesy of John A. Pawloski.)

This 1840s photograph shows the open pit operation of Connecticut's largest and richest copper mine located in Bristol. The deposit was discovered in the 1790s; shafts were eventually dug into the ore to a depth of 600 feet. This view shows an open pit operation, prior to mining underground. (Courtesy of the Bristol Library and Historical Society.)

Between 1847 and 1854, nearly 1,811 tons of copper were removed from the Bristol Copper Mine, netting the owners $197,320. The property frequently changed ownership, but the operations never achieved the profits previously cited. This 1930s photograph shows the inclined track leading from the mine hoisting building. (Courtesy of Frederick Chesson, photograph by Charles R. Harte.)

The mine hoisting building is seen in this 1930s photograph of the Bristol Copper Mine. There were several vertical shafts dug into the ore deposit, and these shafts were connected by tunnels called drifts. Some shafts were used for raising and lowering men and materials while other shafts were for air circulation. The mine closed in 1895. (Courtesy of Frederick Chesson, photograph by Charles R. Harte.)

This is the adit, or entrance, to the Tallman Copper Mine in Hamden of which little information is known. Most of the Connecticut copper mines occur in the sedimentary rocks of the early Jurassic Period. This photograph was taken in 1943. (Courtesy of Frederick Chesson, photograph by Charles R. Harte.)

This 1943 photograph shows the interior of the Tallman Copper Mine in Hamden, which had many horizontal tunnels called drifts. There are no supporting timbers seen in this photograph. Miners would drive their tunnels following the main ore vein until the ore ran out or became economically unfeasible to work. (Courtesy of Frederick Chesson, photograph by Charles R. Harte.)

This *c.* 1870 photograph is reported to be of the Jinny Hill Mine, Cheshire; the first barite mine in the United States. The refined barite was primarily used in the manufacture of paint. The barite mine shafts went to 600 feet, and had several miles of drifts. The Jinny Hill Mine opened in 1837, and produced 160,000 tons of barite in its 40 year history. (Courtesy of the Cheshire Historical Society.)

CHESHIRE HISTORICAL SOCIETY
BICENTENNIAL, 1976

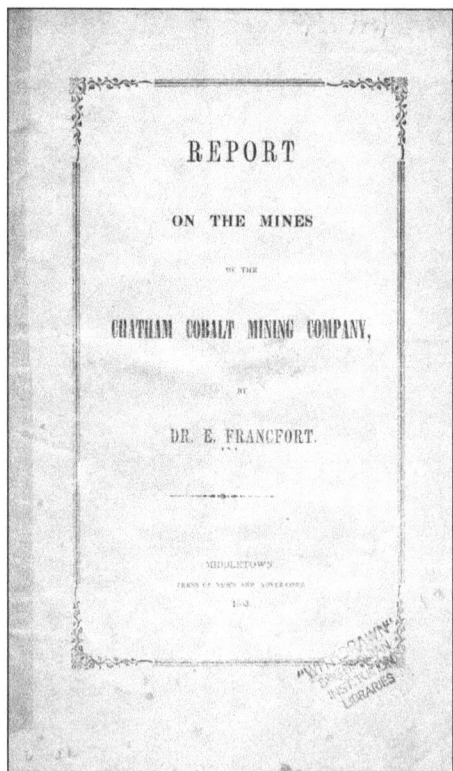

REPORT

ON THE MINES

OF THE

CHATHAM COBALT MINING COMPANY,

BY

DR. E. FRANCFORT.

MIDDLETOWN
PRINTED BY NEWS AND ADVERTISER
1863.

The town of Cobalt (Chatham) is honored for having the first cobalt and the first nickel mines in North America. Gov. John Winthrop Jr. mined gold from the site in the 1660s. One hundred years later, cobalt and nickel ores were discovered there, but most of the mining took place in the 1850s. Most of the cobalt ore was shipped to Philadelphia and to China for use as a dark blue pottery glaze. (Courtesy of John A. Pawloski.)

It was discovered that the cobalt ore contained about 50 percent nickel. To obtain these ores, several shafts were dug, some to a depth of 120 feet. Drifts were blasted through the rock to connect several of these shafts. An elaborate mill was constructed to process the ore. The mines closed in the late 1850s. This 1944 photograph is of the Brook Tunnel in Cobalt. (Courtesy of Frederick Chesson, photograph by Charles R. Harte.)

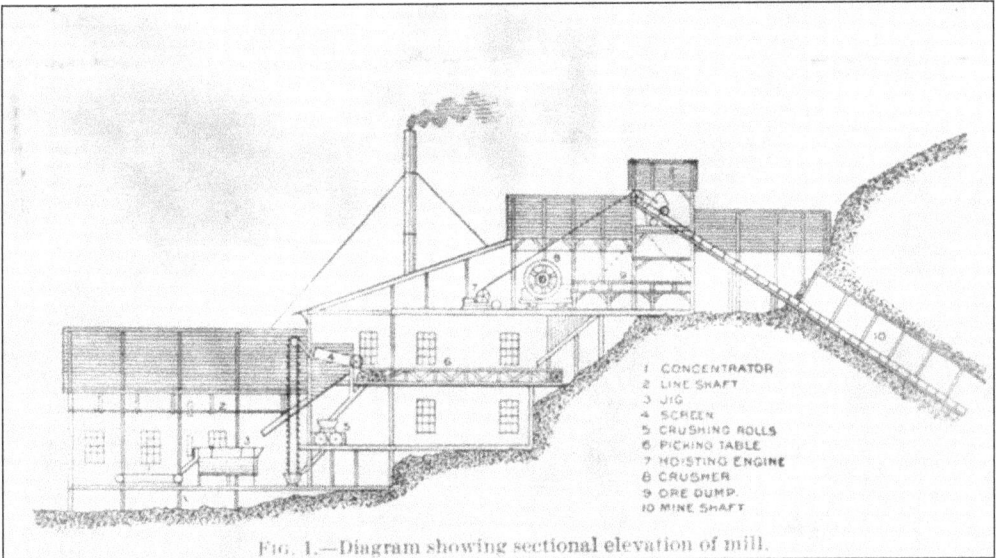

1 CONCENTRATOR
2 LINE SHAFT
3 JIG
4 SCREEN
5 CRUSHING ROLLS
6 PICKING TABLE
7 HOISTING ENGINE
8 CRUSHER
9 ORE DUMP.
10 MINE SHAFT

FIG. 1.—Diagram showing sectional elevation of mill.

The present day Old Mine Park in Trumbull is the site of the first tungsten mine in North America, and mining at this site began in 1803 for lime. Tungsten has been known to exist on the property since 1818. In 1897, the Rare Metals Company of New Jersey sank two inclined shafts into the hillside and constructed an elaborate mill. This drawing shows a cross section of the mill. (Courtesy of Frederick Chesson from Hobbs, 1901, photograph by Charles R. Harte.)

The Rare Metals Company of New Jersey mine was closed in 1901 because of difficulties in removing sulfide minerals from the tungsten ore. The Bethlehem Steel Company took over the operations, and changes were made in the concentrating plant and mining resumed. The mine closed after only eight months of operation. This view of the concentrating mill was taken from the north. (Courtesy of Frederick Chesson from Hobbs, 1901, photograph by Charles R. Harte.)

In 1912, Frederick C. Beach purchased the tungsten mine complex and organized it into the Long Hill Mining Company. This view of the tungsten concentrating mill was taken prior to 1916, when a mysterious fire destroyed all of the buildings. (Courtesy of Frederick Chesson from Hobbs, 1901, photograph by Charles R. Harte.)

Four

PEGMATITE MINING
FROM GEMSTONES TO
POULTRY GRIT

Pegmatites have been mined in Connecticut since 1825. Pegmatite is defined as an intrusive igneous rock, which means it was once hot molten rock forced into cracks or between layers of rock where it slowly cooled and formed large crystals. It is a fact some of the largest crystals in the world come from pegmatite; beryl to 30 feet, spodumene to 10 feet, and quartz to six feet. The primary minerals that make up pegmatite are quartz, feldspar, and mica, although associated minerals can widely vary depending upon the chemical makeup of the magma. Each pegmatite can be valuable in its own way.

The basic pegmatite minerals of quartz, feldspar, and mica are industrially more significant than others since they are more abundant.

Pegmatite quarries are found scattered throughout much of Connecticut, but most are found concentrated in a belt approximately one mile wide and nine miles long from Glastonbury to Haddam, which is known as the Middletown Pegmatite District. The quarries of the Middletown Pegmatite District have produced the most feldspar, mica, and accessory minerals. Other important pegmatite operations were located in Southford, Branchville, and New Milford.

The first new mineral ever to be discovered in the United States, columbite, was identified in 1802, and the new element columbium, came from it. The specimen was actually found in the late 1600s and given to Gov. John Winthrop Jr., who sent it to Sir Hans Sloane of the Royal Society of England. The specimen is believed to have come from the Tollgate Pegmatite in Middletown.

The Branchville Quarry, located in the town of Redding, is world famous for the eight new phosphate minerals discovered there; eosphorite, triploidite, dickinsonite, natrophilite, lithiophilite, reddingite, fairfieldite, and fillowite.

Also found in pegmatite are Connecticut's best gemstones; green and pink tourmalines and clear, pink, green, yellow, and blue beryl.

The last pegmatite operation in Connecticut ceased operations on January 1, 1991.

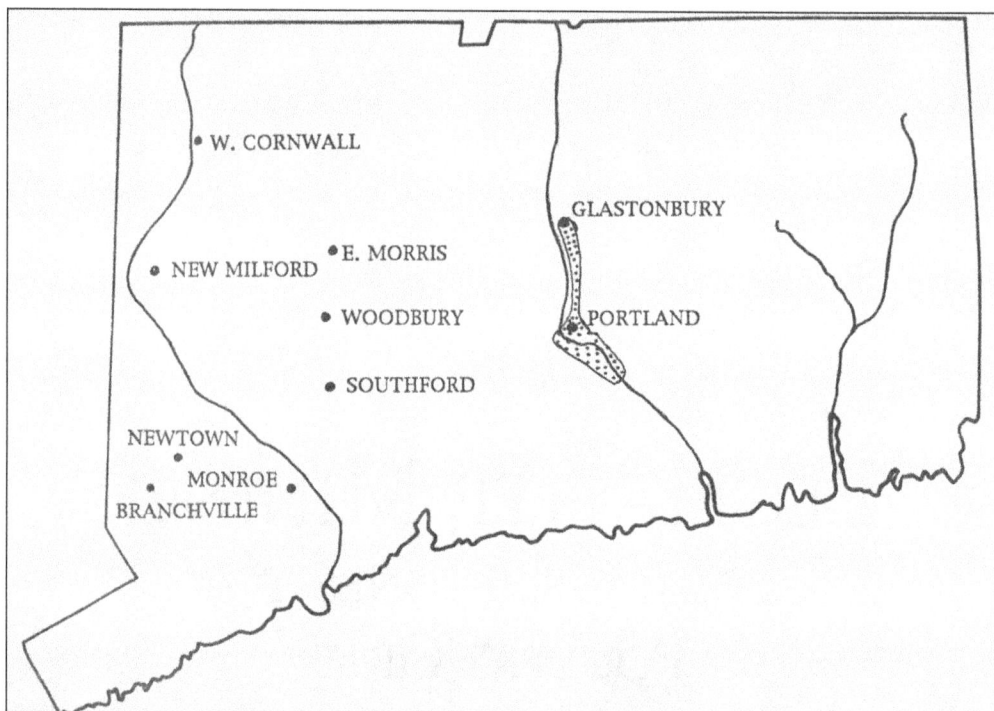

This map shows the distribution of the major pegmatite quarries in Connecticut. Dozens of other smaller quarries and prospects can be found scattered throughout eastern and western Connecticut. The shaded area represents the Middletown Pegmatite District. (Created by John A. Pawloski.)

The dumps, or waste rock piles, of the Strickland and Eureka quarries can be seen in this photograph. The Strickland Quarry is located on Collins Hill in Portland and mining first began in the 1840s. In 1906, the Eureka Mining and Operating Company opened a second pit just east of the Strickland operation. This photograph was taken in 1943. (Courtesy of Frederick Chesson, photograph by Charles R. Harte.)

This north looking view of the Strickland-Eureka quarries, photographed in 1943, nicely illustrates the white rock of the pegmatite ore body that was intruded into the darker surrounding rock. In the late 1930s, a drift was penetrated into the north end of the quarry to remove the best ore. The pit was over 180 feet deep at the north end. (Courtesy of Frederick Chesson, photograph by Charles R. Harte.)

Another view of the Strickland-Eureka quarries shows the north drift and two smaller drifts in the west wall of the pit. Feldspar, the main ore, was used primarily in the porcelain industry. Quartz was mined for the glass and abrasive industry, and mica for electrical insulators. Several pockets of gem tourmalines were encountered during mining, which ceased in the 1950s. (Courtesy of Frederick Chesson, photograph by Charles R. Harte.)

The Gillette Quarry, located in Haddam Neck, is one of the most famous mineral localities in the United States. The mine was started by M. P. Gillette in 1896 for gem tourmalines, mineral specimens, and commercial grade feldspar. This 1890s view shows a miner drilling into the floor of the quarry in preparation for blasting, and the Gillette homestead can be seen above the quarry. (Courtesy of Donald Hindle, John A. Pawloski collection.)

M. P. Gillette and his wife are seated by their house adjacent to the quarry in this 1890s photograph. The Gillette Quarry is world famous for the gem tourmalines found there. From 1905 to 1909, the American Gem Company, an affiliate of Tiffany's of New York City, leased the quarry to mine for gemstones. (Courtesy of Don Hindle, John A. Pawloski collection.)

During World War II, many of the abandoned mines and quarries were reopened for the strategic minerals needed for the war effort, and during the war, Connecticut pegmatite quarries were primarily mined for mica and beryl. This 1940s view of the Gillette Quarry shows miners preparing a scoop for hoisting rock. (Courtesy of the Connecticut Museum of Mining and Mineral Science.)

In this 1940s photograph of the Gillette Quarry, miners are loading the scoop to haul rock from the pit. The area in shadow is a drift where high grade ore was mined. The ore was separated from the waste rock by breaking away the bad parts with a hammer, which is called hand cobbing. The waste rock was then removed from the pit with the derrick. (Courtesy of the Connecticut Museum of Mining and Mineral Science.)

53

Pegmatite quarries are usually long and narrow, as seen in this 1940s photograph of the Gillette Quarry. The depth of the quarry depended upon the quality of the ore, and in many cases, the amount of ground water coming into the pit. Notice the crude ladder used by the miners to gain access to the lower level of the quarry. (Courtesy of the Connecticut Museum of Mining and Mineral Science.)

Around 1900, the Consolidated Feldspar Mill was constructed at the base of the White Rocks Quarry in Middletown. The better grade feldspar was used for pottery, and the lesser grades for asphalt shingles and poultry grit. The last owner of the quarry and mill was the Feldspar Corporation of North Carolina who closed it in 1991, the last pegmatite operation in Connecticut. These storage bins are now gone. (Courtesy of the Feldspar Corporation, John A. Pawloski collection.)

The Eureka Mining and Operating Company of Trenton, New Jersey, began quarrying pegmatite in Cornwall in the early 1900s, when this photograph was taken. The mined feldspar was shipped by rail to New Jersey and used in making porcelain. The sign states "no trespassing." (Courtesy of the Cornwall Historical Society.)

The Cornwall pegmatite deposit is located on the top of the hill on the right side of this early-1900s photograph. The dump pile is behind the first pole on the right. The cobbed feldspar was shoveled down a wide chute to the trestle where it was shoveled into wheelbarrows for loading into the rail cars. (Courtesy of the Cornwall Historical Society.)

The Roebling Mine, located in New Milford, was mined for mica, feldspar, and gem beryl between 1840 and 1900. The mine remained idle until 1944, when it was reopened for mica only. The Roebling Mine is world famous for the quality of golden beryl (heliodor) found in the 1890s. This is the only known photograph of the Roebling Mine taken when gems were being mined in the 1890s. (Courtesy of John A. Pawloski, photograph by Clarence Evans.)

HUNTING MILLIONS

AMERICA'S GEM STONE
IS GOLDEN BERYL

VERY RARE

In the 1950s and 1960s, Howard Hewett operated the Roebling Mine in New Milford and the Turkey Hill Quarry in Haddam, primarily for gemstone mining. This photograph is of an advertising poster for Hewitt's gems featuring garnets and beryl in rough and finished forms. (Courtesy of John A. Pawloski.)

The quarry men in this 1890s photograph are drilling into a pegmatite in Glastonbury. The miner (back row, second from right) is standing next to a "widow maker," which is a rock drill that does not feed water through the drill to suppress the stone dust. A miner could develop a lung disease called silicosis from breathing in too much of this dust. (Courtesy of Frederick Chesson, photograph by Charles R. Harte.)

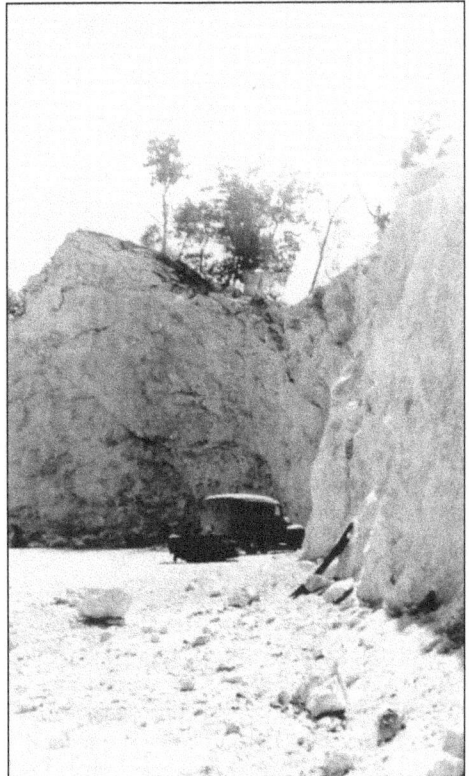

This photograph was taken in 1948 of the Husband Feldspar Quarry in South Glastonbury. The feldspar for the Husband quarry was used in the ceramics industry and also as the abrasive in Bon Ami soap and cleanser that "hasn't scratched yet." The ore from this quarry was transported to the Howe Feldspar mill three miles away for grinding. (Courtesy of Frederick Chesson, photograph by Charles R. Harte.)

The Bridgeport Wood Finishing Quarry in Southford opened in 1906 and was mined for quartz and feldspar. The ore was shipped by rail to their mill in New Milford. The feldspar went to ceramic manufacturers while the quartz was ground into abrasives and was used as filler in paint. In the 1950s and 1960s, the quarry was mined for beryl. This 1960s photograph shows Alton Urban removing a beryl crystal. (Courtesy of Alton Urban.)

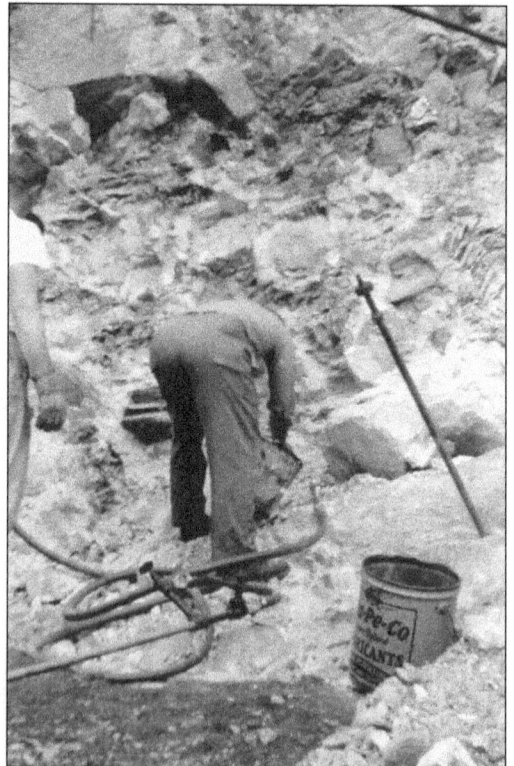

Alton Urban is seen in this 1960s photograph removing a 24 inch diameter beryl crystal from the quarry. Numerous other large hexagonal shaped beryl crystals can be seen in the quarry wall. Beryl became a strategic mineral during the cold war, and was stockpiled by the federal government. (Courtesy of Alton Urban.)

Most of the feldspar mined in Connecticut was crushed, ground, and bagged prior to shipping to the manufacturer. This photograph, taken in the early 1900s, shows the interior of a Glastonbury feldspar mill. After the ore was crushed to the size of a pea, it was then shoveled beneath the moving stone mill wheels to be pulverized. Once the ground feldspar passed through a sieve, it was then bagged for shipping. The size of the finished feldspar particle was determined by what it was to be used for. Poultry grit was the size of a sand grain, while the ceramics industry used flour sized particles. (Courtesy of Frederick Chesson, Charles R. Harte collection.)

Glastonbury can boast of having the first feldspar mill in North America, which was built in 1825. It was standard practice at the time for mills to be built on a stream in order to power the machinery. This early-1900s photograph is of the Wiarda Feldspar Mill in South Glastonbury. (Courtesy of Frederick Chesson, Charles R. Harte collection.)

The Connecticut feldspar industry saw a slow but steady increase from 700 tons annual production in 1837, to 19,043 tons in 1907. In 1908, Connecticut was the number one producer of feldspar in the United States. Charles R. Harte took this photograph of the Eureka Milling Company Portland plant in 1944. (Courtesy of Frederick Chesson.)

Mica is prized for its high electrical and heat resistance, and its uses consist of electrical capacitors and insulators, stove and furnace windows, non-electrical conducting dry lubricant, and as the sparkle in toothpaste, plastics, and the glitter in make up. Most of the quality mica mined in Connecticut came from the Strickland-Eureka Quarry and the Roebling Mine. This 1940s photograph shows some of the large "books" of mica mined in Connecticut. (Courtesy of Frederick Chesson, Charles R. Harte collection.)

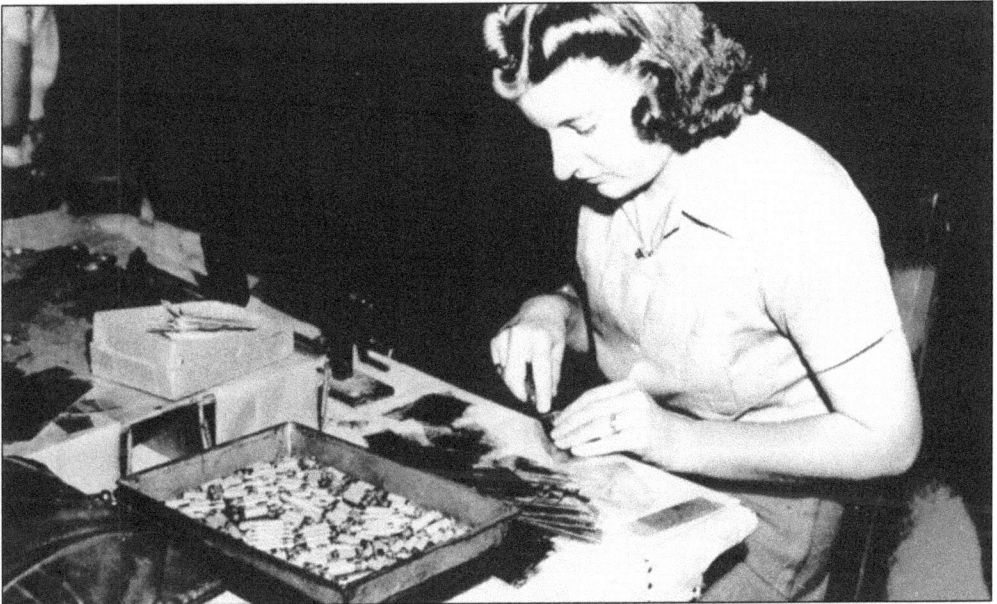

Before mica is manufactured into its various products, it is sorted by size and quality. Its use as an electronics insulator demands that it be of the best quality. One of the physical properties of mica is that it can be easily split into thin sheets as seen in this picture. Once the sheets are split they can then be punched out into the desired shapes. This photograph is from a 1940s Connecticut Economic Development Commission bulletin. (Courtesy of Frederick Chesson, Charles R. Harte collection.)

The world's largest single deposit of quartz is Lantern Hill in North Stonington. Mining of silex, as quartz is sometimes called, began at Lantern Hill in the early 1870s. The quartz was hauled by wagon to Mystic where it was ground, loaded onto ships, and sent to New Jersey pottery works. The person near the center of the picture is drilling holes for blasting. (Courtesy of Frederick Chesson, Charles R. Harte collection.)

This early postcard view can lead one to believe that the Lantern Hill Quarry was in Rhode Island, when it is actually in Connecticut. In 1890, the deposit and plant were sold to a Mr. Seely, a paint manufacturer, who operated the business until the plant burned in 1913. In 1916, the Connecticut Silica Company was formed and a new mill constructed. (Courtesy of John A. Pawloski.)

62

This 1966 photograph of Lantern Hill was taken when the mine was owned by the Ottawa Silica Company. A large steel ball was dropped from the crane to break up the larger pieces of blasted quartz. This technique is still used in many quarries today. (Courtesy of the U.S. Silica Company.)

This undated photograph is a view of the Lantern Hill mill taken from the south. In 1935, the Connecticut Silica Company merged with the North American Silica Company. The company went into bankruptcy soon after the merger. In 1939, the Lantern Hill Silica Company was formed and mined the deposit. (Courtesy of the U.S. Silica Company.)

On December 8, 1963, a fire destroyed the Ottawa Silica Company mill in North Stonington. In 1966, a new mill was built at the Lantern Hill quarry. In 1987, the Rio Tinto Zinc Company of England purchased the Ottawa Silica Company and formed the U.S. Silica division. (Courtesy of U.S. Silica Company.)

This 1992 photograph of the U.S. Silica Company's Lantern Hill operation shows a large stockpile of ground quartz. Much of the milled quartz was used in the manufacture of glass. The aggregate facing of the John F. Kennedy Library in Boston came from Lantern Hill. In 1994, the Mashantucket-Pequot Tribal Nation purchased the U.S. Silica operation. (Photograph by John A. Pawloski.)

The largest and most elaborate quartz, or silica mill, was constructed in 1882 by the Bridgeport Wood Finishing Company at the confluence of the Still and Housatonic Rivers in New Milford. Wheeler's patented Wood Filler, Breining's Oil Stain, and Breining's Lithogen Silicate Paint were the main products produced in this plant. The Bridgeport Wood Finishing Company letterhead in this illustration is dated 1897. (Courtesy of John A. Pawloski.)

The construction of the Bridgeport Wood Finishing Company main building in New Milford was quite an undertaking, as can be seen in this 1882 photograph. To install the water turbine, the Housatonic River, seen at the bottom of photograph, had to be diverted. The large building under construction housed the crushing and sifting operations. (Courtesy of Robin Stack.)

This is a close up view of the water turbine power building and millrace around 1910, when repairs were being made to the Bridgeport Wood Finishing Company's New Milford plant. Belts connected the turbine to pulleys on a line shaft that ran the length of the building, and additional belts came off the line shaft to power individual machines. (Courtesy of Robin Stack.)

This photograph of the main building of the Bridgeport Wood Finishing Company's New Milford operation was taken sometime after the plant was rebuilt, after a devastating fire in 1902 destroyed the original structure. A wing dam was used for diverting a portion of the Housatonic to the turbine. The wing dam can be seen in the foreground. (Courtesy of Robin Stack.)

An aerial photograph, taken around 1920 of the Bridgeport Wood Finishing Company's New Milford operation, shows the relationship of the river, mill race, main plant, and other buildings of the company. In 1917, the paint and wood filler division was sold to the E. I. DuPont Company, which fairly quickly phased out the operation. (Courtesy of John A. Pawloski.)

This early postcard photograph of the Bridgeport Wood Finishing Company's New Milford plant, taken after the 1902 fire, shows piles of quartz ore brought by rail from the company owned quarry located in Southford. The ground quartz was also used in abrasives for polishing, in hand soaps, and for making grinding wheels. (Courtesy of John A. Pawloski.)

The Bridgeport Wood Finishing Company used silica buhr stone wheels to finely grind the quartz down. As the silica wheels became worn down in the grinding process, they became part of the product. This c. 1910 photograph shows three workers hand drilling the bearing hole in a new wheel. (Courtesy of Robin Stack.)

Two buhr stone wheels with bearings in place can be seen in this photograph taken around 1910. The wheels were approximately five feet in diameter when new, and were replaced when they were worn down to about 30 inches. The stones were usually made from either a quartz conglomerate or a fossiliferous chalcedony. (Courtesy of Robin Stack.)

The Bridgeport Wood Finishing Company used screens of woven silk to sift the pulverized quartz. The main reason for using silk is because it would last longer than metal screens, and it would not contaminate the product with metal. This photograph, taken around 1910, shows barrels of the ground silica that have been prepared for shipping. (Courtesy of Robin Stack.)

The Bridgeport Wood Finishing Company operated a second mill and several quarries in the Branchville section of Redding. The quarries were located within a few miles of the Branchville plant. This photograph was taken in the early 1900s. (Courtesy of John A. Pawloski.)

This *c.* 1900 view shows most of the Bridgeport Wood Finishing Company's Branchville plant. Large stockpiles of white quartz can be seen around the building. The quartz ore was trammed up the ramp to an annealing kiln before it went into the processing mill. Annealing made the quartz easier to pulverize. (Courtesy of John A. Pawloski.)

Five

BUILDING STONE
THE FOUNDATION
OF CIVILIZATION

The building and monumental stone industry is quite different from other mining industries. It is not directed towards the blasting and crushing of the rock into tiny pieces so that the valuable ore can be separated from the waste rock. The building industry requires an attractive, durable rock of larger size which can be stacked together in order to construct buildings, or sawed into slabs, polished, and used on the facades of buildings. These same types of rock can be shaped, polished, and inscribed as monuments.

In this regard, Connecticut also played the leading role in the development of this phase of the mining industry by having the first granite quarry (1648), the first sandstone quarry (1639), the first systematic quarrying and milling of marble (pre-1800), and the first verde antique quarry (1811).

The verde antique from Milford was prized throughout the country, and its most distinguished use was in several carved fireplaces, which decorated the United States Capital and the East Room of the White House in Washington, D.C.

Most building stone is mined from open pits called quarries. The actual methods vary with the size of the operation and the available technology during that time in history. Initially the deposit provided rock that could be removed using pry bars and wedges.

In all mining operations, holes must be drilled into the rock either for blasting or for splitting. All drilling was done by hand prior to the invention of the pneumatic rock drill in the 1880s, but hand drilling is a slow and arduous process, and miners were quick to adapt to the use of pneumatic drills if they could afford them.

In many instances, larger quarry operations also had carving and finishing shops. Once again, the finishing process depended upon the finances of the company and the technology available at the time. Initially all carving and polishing was done with hand tools, while today pneumatic tools, sand blasting, lasers, and diamond grinders are employed.

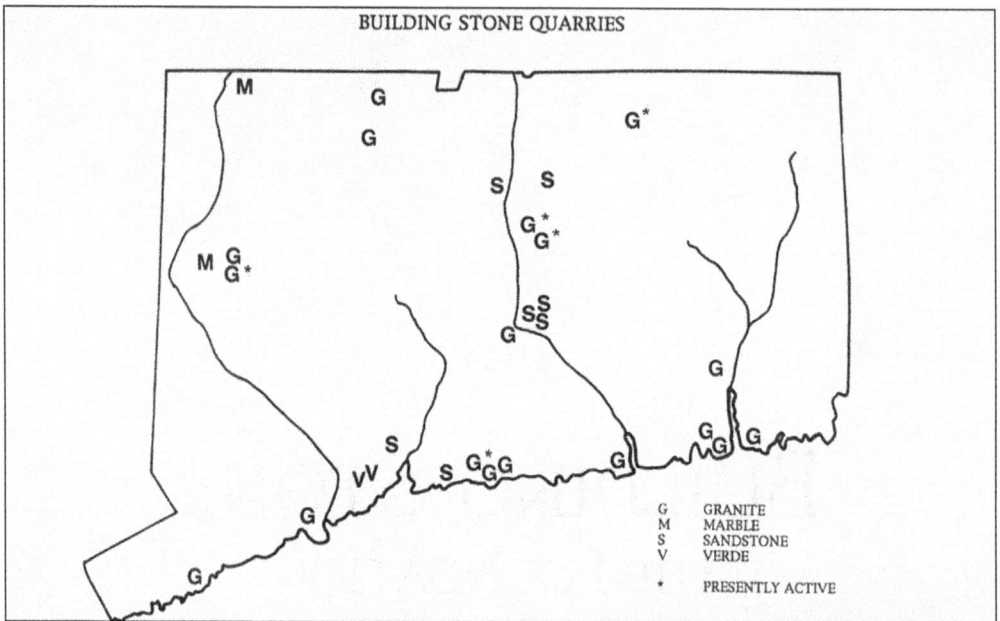

G	GRANITE
M	MARBLE
S	SANDSTONE
V	VERDE
*	PRESENTLY ACTIVE

One will notice from this map that there is a pattern to the locations of the different building stone. Marble is found in the western part of Connecticut, while the sandstone occurs mainly in the central portion of the state. Granite and granite gneiss is found almost everywhere else, but most of the granite quarries are located along the southern boundary of the state. (Created by John A. Pawloski.)

This small operating stone quarry in New Milford uses a hand-operated winch on a swivel derrick to hoist the blocks of stone onto a wagon pulled by a team of horses. Stone from this type of local quarry was used for foundations, flagging, curbing, and fireplace hearths. (Courtesy of John A. Pawloski.)

This 1944 photograph shows the north end of the Millstone granite quarry in Waterford. The Millstone Quarry, developed by John Winthrop Jr. in 1648, was the first granite quarry in the colonies and was used for making millstones. Millstone became the largest of all granite quarries in Connecticut and was operated almost continuously for 315 years. (Courtesy of Frederick Chesson, photograph by Charles R. Harte.)

This 1944 photograph is of a stiff-legged derrick on the east side of the Millstone Quarry. A stiff-legged derrick was good for hoisting large blocks of rock out of the quarry, but did not permit much side-to-side motion. By 1847, the Millstone Quarry was shipping 30,000 tons of granite per year, mostly to markets in New York City; Philadelphia, Pennsylvania; and Charleston, South Carolina. (Courtesy of Frederick Chesson, photograph by Charles R. Harte.)

A vertical quarry drill is being used to bore holes in the granite. There are two hoses leading to this drill. One is for the air supply to power the drill, and the second hose is to provide a stream of water to cool the drill, flush out the rock chips, and to suppress dust. This photograph was taken in the 1950s. (Courtesy of Dante Tedali.)

A rail mounted steam derrick is utilized to move the quarried rocks around in the Millstone Quarry stone yard as seen in this 1920s photograph. By using a mobile crane, the heavy blocks of stone could be moved around with ease. In good weather, stone cutters and finishers could work outside. (Courtesy of Dante Tedali.)

Stone workers can be seen facing large blocks of granite at the Millstone Quarry yard in Waterford. A rail mounted steam derrick can be seen in the background of this 1920s photograph. At the peak of the Millstone operation, during the early 1900s, as many as 800 men were employed here. A company town, Graniteville, was established to service the workers and their families. (Courtesy of Dante Tedali.)

A 1920s stone worker is seen facing a block of granite using a hammer and a chisel at the Millstone Quarry yard. There are special hammers and special chisels used in the dressing of stone. The smaller pieces of stone were made into paving blocks, and the chips were crushed into aggregate. (Courtesy of Dante Tedali.)

75

By the early 1900s, pneumatic tools were quickly replacing the hand tools of the stone worker. This 1920s photograph shows a pneumatic facing machine being used at the Millstone Quarry stone yard. The Millstone Quarry employed seven blacksmiths to keep the tools sharp and to maintain the equipment. (Courtesy of Dante Tedali.)

Another Proof of "Fine Grain and Good CONTRAST" in

BLUE MILLSTONE GRANITE

Substituted in "BRONZE TABLETS" ordered

The tablet illustrated was one of two originally ordered in Bronze to mark the "Queens Midtown Tunnel." Bronze priorities enabled the contractors, the D. J. Tedaldi Construction Company of Bronx, N. Y., to suggest Granite and the order was given the Bottinelli Monumental Company of New London, Conn., who used Millstone Blue Granite for its extra fine grain and excellent contrast absolutely necessary for detail as the small letters are only 3/8" high. The Tunnel Authorities were very pleased with the result.

Attention Lithichrome Users

Millstone Dark Pink with its fine contrast and delicate pastel tone is an ideal Medium for the finest Lithichrome work.

The Millstone Operating Corporation

JAMES E. RANTA, Manager

QUARRIERS AND MANUFACTURERS - MILLSTONE, CONN.

MILLSTONE GRANITE DARK LIGHT BLUE or PINK

A 1950s advertisement proclaims the quality of the Millstone granite. The granite from the Millstone Quarry was primarily sent to New York City and was used in the construction of the Cloisters, Grand Central Station, and the foundations of the United Nations Building. It was also used in the making of Grand Square in Mexico City, the foundation of Fort Sumter, and the older buildings at West Point. (Courtesy of Dante Tedali.)

In this c. 1900 photograph, the workers, in an unidentified Branford quarry, show that it was a fairly large operation. Judging from the number of quarrymen holding sledge hammers it seems to indicate that drilling at this quarry was by hand. Most quarries are worked in steps called benches, and the height of each bench was determined by the natural layering of the rock. (Courtesy of the Branford Historical Society.)

The Stony Creek Quarry in North Branford was opened by the Norcross brothers in 1887. This quarry is famous for its pink colored granite, and is still in operation today. One remarkable monumental piece from the Stony Creek Quarry was a 45 foot tall by six foot square obelisk weighing 60 tons made from a single piece of granite This photograph, taken in 1993, shows a stiff-legged derrick above the pit. (Photograph by John A. Pawloski.)

Stone carvers or stone finishers are seen in this early-1900s photograph, at an unidentified Branford quarry, carving the molded edge on granite foundation blocks. The derricks seen in the background are for moving the blocks of stone around the yard. Most of the Connecticut quarrymen were English, Nordic, or Italian immigrants. (Courtesy of the Branford Historical Society.)

78

A beautifully carved block of granite from an unidentified Branford quarry is having the upper surface finished. The stone workers are using flat-edged hammers, called bush hammers, to smooth the surface. It is interesting to note that the granite used to make the base of the Statue of Liberty came from Leet's Island Quarry in Guilford and the Hoadley Quarry in Branford. (Courtesy of the Branford Historical Society.)

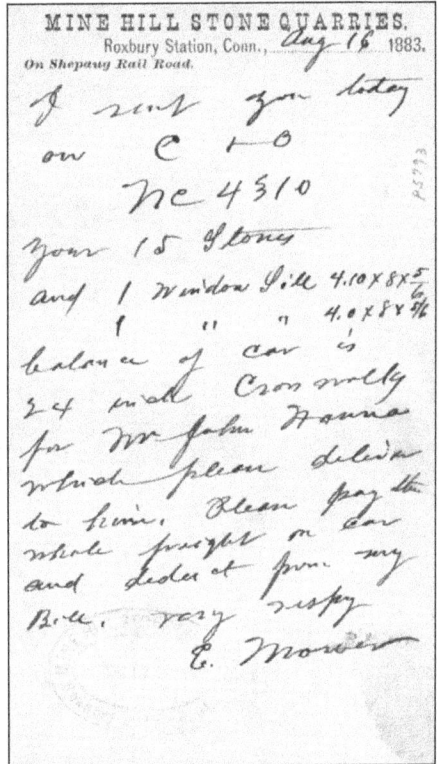

The stone at the Mine Hill Quarry, Roxbury is primarily fine-grained granite gneiss, which is well suited for producing large dimension stones. Stone was being quarried at Mine Hill as early as 1837. This early postal card is an order confirmation of a stone shipment to the New Britain Lumber and Coal Company, and is dated August 16, 1883. (Courtesy of John A. Pawloski.)

MINE HILL QUARRY, ROXBURY, CONN.

The Mine Hill Quarry later became the Rockside Quarry. The owners boasted that they could produce stone six feet wide by 60 feet long, one foot thick! This c. 1900 postcard shows the stone yard of the Rockside Quarry. The construction of the Shepaug Railroad adjacent to the quarry helped with its financial success. (Courtesy of John A. Pawloski.)

Much of the stone quarried at Mine Hill was shipped by rail to Bridgeport and then by barge to New York City. Mine Hill granite was used in the construction of the East River Bridge and the 1,350 foot long, 58 feet high, and 21 feet thick retaining wall between 67th and 72nd Streets in New York City. (Courtesy of John A. Pawloski, photograph by Joseph West.)

This 1906 photograph shows the railroad loading platforms for a second granite quarry on the top of Mine Hill. The stone was brought downhill to the loading area by a dual track inclined rail system. As the car loaded with stone went down to the loading area, it pulled an empty car up hill to the quarry. The conical structures in the background are stone charcoal kilns. (Courtesy of John A. Pawloski, photograph by Joseph West.)

The quarrymen in this photograph can be seen breaking off large blocks of granite using feathers and wedges at the Rockside Quarry, Roxbury. Pneumatic drills were used for drilling, and steam powered derricks were used for moving the blocks to the stone yard. The Rockside quarrying operation closed around 1935, but the upper quarry at Mine Hill is still being worked. This photograph was taken in 1906 by Joseph West. (Courtesy of John A. Pawloski.)

The first commercial quarrying of stone in North America began at Hartford in 1639 and it was a form of sandstone, which was reddish-brown and nicknamed brownstone, that was found throughout the central part of the state. Little is known about the Hartford quarry; however, those in Portland, once called Chatham, are well documented. This illustration is a 1788 advertisement for the Shaler and Hall Quarry in Portland. (Courtesy of Frederick Chesson, Charles R. Harte collection.)

This late 1800s illustration of the Brainerd Quarry, formerly owned by Shaler and Hall, in Portland shows a swivel derrick (upper left) and two stiff-legged derricks, all powered by steam hoists. A special stone wagon drawn by a team of oxen can be seen in the insert illustration. (Courtesy of John A. Pawloski.)

The Connecticut Free Stone Quarry Company,

of Cromwell, Middlesex Co., Connecticut.

Sold to *Archibald Murray*

ROBINSON GILL, President.
FRANK W. BLISS, Secretary.
OLIVER W. MACK, Treas. and Manager.

May 2d 1896.

1895				
Nov 19	1 Dbl Load Rubble	1 80		
1896 20	1	1 80	3 60	
May 2	4 Cellar Steps 4-ea = 16."	30	4 80	
	Paid May. 2d 1896.		8 40	
	Frank W. Bliss Secretary			

The Connecticut Free Stone Quarry was located in Cromwell. This bill, dated May 2, 1896, is for a load of rubble and four cellar steps. Most of the brownstone was used in the famous "brownstone" buildings in New York City. When brownstone was in vogue as a building stone, Connecticut was the source used by builders throughout Europe and North America. (Courtesy of John A. Pawloski.)

This photograph, taken in the late 1800s of the Brainerd Quarry in Portland, shows its proximity to the Connecticut River, which was used for shipping the finished brownstone. In the early 1880s, when brownstone was popular in architecture, the quarries employed over 1,500 men, 100 teams of oxen, and a fleet of 50 schooners. (Courtesy of Frederick Chesson, Charles R. Harte collection.)

Steam powered channeling machines can be seen in the lower left corner of this photograph. A channeling machine is a specialized track mounted pneumatic chisel that cuts a groove in the rock so it will break along a straight line. (Courtesy of Frederick Chesson, Charles R. Harte collection.)

This postcard photograph of a Portland brownstone quarry is dated 1911. Access to this area of the quarry was by ladder. The quarrymen in this photograph are seen drilling vertical holes for the feather and wedging process to split off a large block of stone. Stone was usually quarried in a step-like fashion. (Courtesy of John A. Pawloski.)

This 1910 postcard view of a Portland brownstone quarry shows that some of the quarried stone was shipped by railroad. The building in this photograph is an air compressor house. Most quarries used compressed air to power their drills and hoists, but a few quarries used steam instead. (Courtesy of John A. Pawloski.)

An early 1900s postcard view of an abandoned section of a Portland brownstone quarry shows that it does not take long for nature to begin reclaiming the land. A stiff-legged derrick and compressor house can be seen in the center of the photograph.(Courtesy of John A. Pawloski.)

BROWN STONE QUARRY, PORTLAND, CONN.

An operating steam drill can be seen near the center of this 1907 postcard. Most quarries used wooden poles for their derricks. This derrick (left center) is made of steel. Water can be seen in the lower right corner. The Portland brownstone quarries were plagued by the influx of groundwater and had to have pumps running 24 hours per day to keep the flow in under control. (Courtesy of John A. Pawloski.)

Portland, Conn. The Stone Quarry, showing Derricks.

The merger of the Brainerd and Shaler and Hall Quarries in the 1890s was brought about by changing architectural styles in cities, which foretold the demise of the brownstone industry. The traveling cranes in this 1910 postcard view were used for moving large blocks of stone in the Portland stone yard. (Courtesy of John A. Pawloski.)

This early-1880s photograph of a Portland brownstone yard was taken before the advent of mechanical finishing tools and machines. Brownstone was shaped, carved, and smoothed using hand tools. The ethnic makeup of the quarry men in the 1850s was primarily Connecticut residents, but by the 1880s, most quarrymen were Irish immigrants. In 1880, the work day was 10 hours long and quarrymen were paid $1.87 per day. (Courtesy of Frederick Chesson, Charles R. Harte collection.)

Most of the brownstone was shipped by schooner down the Connecticut River and then to ports throughout the world. This late-1890s photograph shows the river front loading area and part of the stone yard. Stone finishing buildings can be seen in the background. (Courtesy of Frederick Chesson, Charles R. Harte collection.)

This 1911 postcard photograph shows a steel derrick being used for loading brownstone onto a schooner at the quarry docks on the Connecticut River in Portland. The river provided a quick and easy means of transportation, and in the 1880s, a fleet of 50 schooners and one steamboat were kept busy supplying the demand for brownstone. (Courtesy of John A. Pawloski.)

A fleet of schooners can be seen at the loading docks of the brownstone quarries in Portland in this c. 1875 photograph. The brownstone quarries were flooded in the spring of 1936, ruining most of the equipment. Attempts were made to restore operations, but unfortunately the quarries were again flooded by the Hurricane of 1938, thus ending 274 years of operation. (Courtesy of Frederick Chesson, Charles R. Harte collection.)

Six

CLAY MINING AND THE BRICK INDUSTRY

At one time, the mining of clay and its use in the manufacture of bricks had a significant impact on the economy and social order of several areas in Connecticut. To understand the significance of the brick industry, it is necessary to develop a historical perspective of life from the early colonies to the present day. The first settlers in an area were most concerned with survival, and manufacturing facilities were nonexistent. The houses they constructed were at first simple wattle and daub structures, having thatched roofs following the tradition of the mother country. Wood burned in fireplaces provided cooking facilities as well as a source of heat. The earliest fireplace chimneys were constructed of either logs covered with clay or stone with a clay binder. Needless to say, these were neither safe nor very stable, and fire was a constant threat.

The first use of bricks in the colonies brought improvement to chimney construction. Its stability increased while the fire risk decreased. But importing the bricks from England was a slow process. So, once the discovery of clay used to make bricks occurred, a new industry grew. For over 100 years, it remained a local industry because heavy, bulky bricks were hard to transport and also brick clay was found in almost every town.

Once the lumber industry began, wood houses, of post and beam construction, replaced the one room waddle and daub style. Many towns became cities, crowded with wooden buildings. Lanterns and candles illuminated the homes, while fireplaces, wood, or coal stoves provided heat. Every city was on borrowed time, for just one careless moment would create an inferno rendering neighborhoods or entire cities in ashes.

City governments concerned with the threat of fire began requiring buildings to be made from bricks. Bricks then became vogue in the cities and remained that way, at least for the common buildings, until the widespread use of steel and concrete took over in the 20th century.

In Connecticut, the brick industry began in Hartford in 1635, and since that time there have been just over 300 brick makers throughout Connecticut's history. Today, only one brick manufacturer survives.

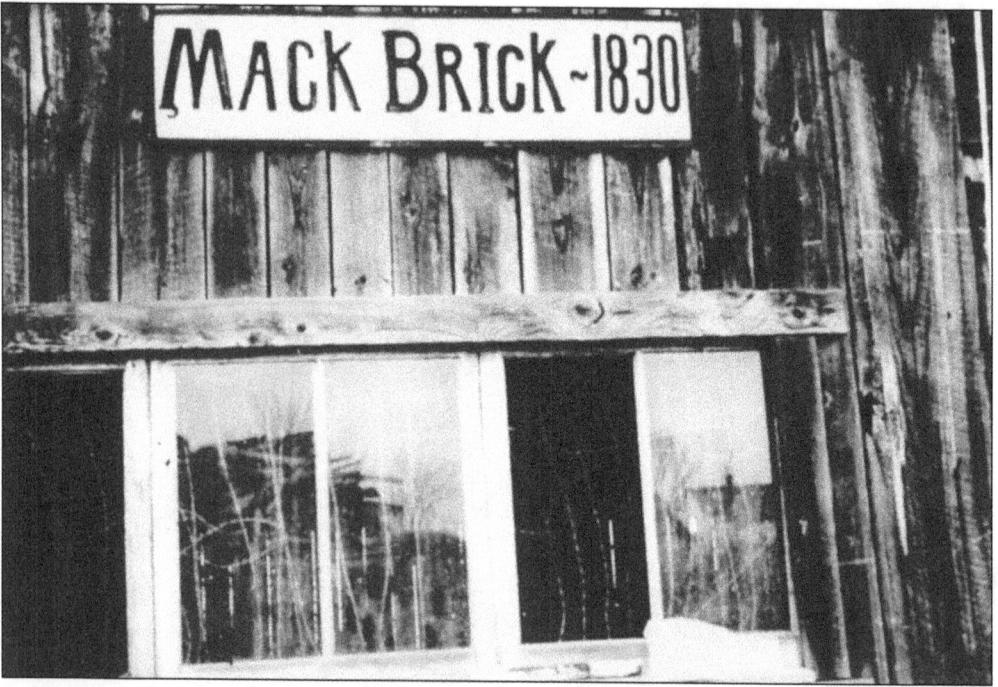

Industrial brick making in the Windsor area began with William Mack in 1830, and was kept in operation by six generations of the family until the plant was sold in 1966. By 1906, the company was producing six million bricks per year. This photograph was taken around 1900. (Courtesy of the Windsor Historical Society.)

This late-1800s photograph of the Mack Brick Yard in Windsor shows the hand molding of brick. Clay, water, and sand are mixed in a pit by a horse turned paddle wheel called a craig. A good brick maker could make about 2,000 bricks per day by hand. (Courtesy of John A. Pawloski.)

These two men are hand molding brick. A brick mold is a form made in the size of the brick to be made, and there may be one to six brick cavities on the form. The brick maker picks up a lump of clay and slams it into the form and then scrapes away the excess material. This c. 1900 photograph is of the Mack Brick Yard in Windsor. (Courtesy of Bo Mack.)

This homemade clay scoop was made by the Mack family and used in their Windsor clay pit in the late 1940s. The double rear tires were needed because the soft slippery clay made traction difficult. (Courtesy of Bo Mack.)

The mined clay went into this homemade dump truck for transporting to the brick yard, where the truck body was then dumped by hand. This c. 1935 photograph was taken at the Mack Brick Yard in Windsor. (Courtesy of Bo Mack.)

In 1797, Dr. Apollos Kinsley, a Connecticut resident, invented the first pressed brick making machine, which made the mass production of a uniformed size brick possible. However, the use of brick machines did not catch on until the 1880s. This 1950s photograph shows a Mack Brick Company employee sliding a mold into the brick machine. (Courtesy of Bo Mack.)

In the brick making process a carrier is a person who takes the molded bricks to the drying area. In this 1950s photograph of the Mack Brick Yard, a carrier has a mold full of bricks to be dumped on to a sandy area to be air dried in preparation for firing in a kiln. The open yard drying method was primarily used by smaller brick companies. (Courtesy of Bo Mack.)

It takes practice to be able to turn over and dump out a mold full of soft bricks without breaking them. The bricks are dried in the sun before they can be stacked into hacks. Special brick barrows were designed to bring the bricks to the drying yard. This is a 1950s photograph of the Mack Brick Yard in Windsor. (Courtesy of Bo Mack.)

Here a clay worker is using an edger to flip six bricks on edge at the same time. The bricks are edged frequently to permit the clay to dry evenly, but one major problem encountered in open yard drying is a heavy rain. This was a nice sunny day at the Mack Brick Yard in the 1950s. (Courtesy of Bo Mack.)

With the threat of bad weather, the newly molded bricks were dumped onto a pallet and the pallets placed on tiers in a drying shed, as seen in the foreground of this 1950s photograph of the Mack Brick Yard. In the background is a scove kiln being constructed from the green (unfired) bricks under the large unroofed building. (Courtesy of Bo Mack.)

For bricks to harden, they need to be baked (fired). The earliest commercial kilns were temporary structures called scove kilns made from the green (unfired) bricks. Arches for the fires are built into the base of the kiln and the outside walls are plastered with mud to make them airtight. In this 1950s photograph, Edward W. Mack III is seen inspecting one of the kilns. (Courtesy of Bo Mack.)

This 1950s view of a fired scove kiln shows the arrangement of bricks that would allow the heat to circulate as evenly as possible during the firing process. The earliest kilns held between 20,000 and 75,000 bricks, later kilns were much larger and contained about 500,000 bricks. After the firing was finished, the bricks were sorted by color and quality. (Courtesy of Bo Mack.)

Little is known of the Johnson Brick Company of Middletown. This bill is dated January 1, 1903. (Courtesy of John A. Pawloski.)

There were a number of brick manufacturers in the Berlin-New Britain area because of the large deposits of good clay found there. The small building seen in this c. 1900 photograph is the office for the American Brick Company in Berlin. (Courtesy of Joan Teske.)

The Donnelly Brick Company in Berlin hauled the clay from the pit to their plant using a Plymouth "dinky" locomotive. One of the rail cars, heaped with clay, is being pulled in this 1930s photograph. The Donnelly Brick Company was one of the largest in Connecticut. (Courtesy of Joan Teske.)

The clay workers of the Merwin Brick Company in Berlin are seen in this c. 1900 photograph. A brick mold is being held by the man in the center, and the left are drying sheds holding pallets of bricks. (Courtesy of Joan Teske.)

This c. 1900 photograph shows a group of clay workers at the Merwin Brick Yard in Berlin. A drying shed holding pallets of bricks can be seen to the right in the photograph. Beginning around 1860, many brick companies would put an identifying mark into their bricks as a form of advertising. Merwin bricks were marked "MERWIN." (Courtesy of Joan Teske.)

Before fork lifts were invented, bricks were loaded onto trucks or into railcars by hand. Fork lifts permitted bricks to be loaded much faster and with much less labor. This is a 1960s view of the Donnelly Brick Yard in Berlin. (Courtesy of Joan Teske.)

This 1902 C. P. Merwin Brick Company, Berlin, letterhead reveals much information. It states that the company was established in 1880, and has the capacity to make 19,000 bricks per day. It manufactured molded and hollow brick as well as building, pallet face, sewer, and paving bricks. If the vignette is accurate we have a good idea of what the plant looked like. (Courtesy of John A. Pawloski.)

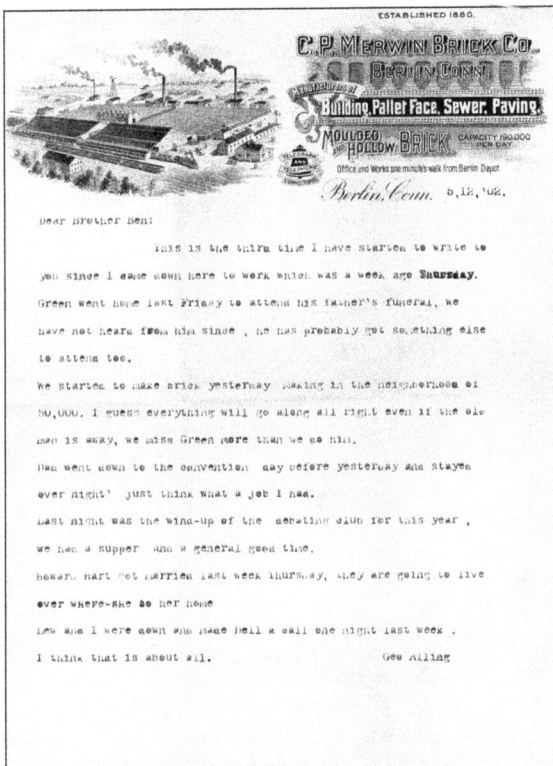

The Stiles family of North Haven was a prominent manufacturer of bricks since the mid-1800s. This photograph, taken around 1910, is of one of the Stiles's clay pits. The workers would use planks to keep the wheelbarrows from sinking into the sticky wet clay. Wagons to haul the clay to the brick plant can be seen in the background. (Courtesy of the North Haven Historical Society.)

This is an 1897 photograph of the I. L. Stiles Brick Company in North Haven. The I. L. Stiles Brick Company was one of the largest and longest lasting brick manufacturers in Connecticut with an annual output of about 12 million bricks. (Courtesy of the North Haven Historical Society.)

This 1904 photograph of an I. L. Stiles clay pit shows how the brick industry was changing. The hand shovel for loading the clay into wagons was replaced by the use of a steam dragline. Notice that the wagons were pulled by both mules and oxen. (Courtesy of the North Haven Historical Society.)

In 1910, the Stiles Brick Company in North Haven was using a narrow gauge steam locomotive to haul cars to and from the clay pits. More clay could be moved using these small railroads than by using draft animals. (Courtesy of the North Haven Historical Society.)

The larger brick manufacturers were producing 30,000 bricks or more per day, but at the time it was not efficient to air dry that quantity, so heated drying buildings were constructed. This photograph, taken around 1950, shows pallets of bricks being placed on the racks in one of the I. L. Stiles steam drying buildings. (Courtesy of the North Haven Historical Society.)

A posed photograph of I. L. Stiles Brick Company workers, taken in 1904, reveals a nice array of specialized wheelbarrows used in the brick industry. The empty barrow (right) is for carrying either dried or fired bricks. The barrow on the left is the identical, but is loaded with bricks. The center barrow was designed to carry pallets of soft brick to the drying area. (Courtesy of the North Haven Historical Society.)

This is an early photograph, from around 1880, of the I. L. Stiles brick yard in North Haven. Pictured in the foreground are the drying areas and covered hacks of stacked green bricks, which are unfired bricks. (Courtesy of the North Haven Historical Society.)

The pit in the foreground is an abandoned cragg, or clay mixing pit. The large building is a covered scove kiln. Hacks of drying bricks can be seen on the left. This photograph is from a stereopticon of the I. L. Stiles Brick Company in North Haven around 1900. (Courtesy of the North Haven Historical Society.)

The clay workers are constructing a 30-arch scove kiln from approximately one million bricks. An arch is where the wood fire is used to bake the bricks. This c. 1900 photograph was taken at the Stiles brick yard in North Haven. (Courtesy of the North Haven Historical Society.)

Seven

LIME AND THE ATOMIC BOMB CONNECTION

One of the earliest and most successful mineral industries in Connecticut was the manufacture of lime from marble. Although there are several major deposits of marble, the primary locus of this industry is the Falls Village-Canaan area. The main belt of marble snakes down western Connecticut from Canaan to Ridgefield, with smaller deposits mined in Trumbull, Woodbridge, and Southington.

The earliest recorded lime operation dates to about 1707 in New Milford, where local farmers constructed small kilns to produce lime for their own use. The oldest commercial manufactory of lime was started by John Read in Redding around 1722.

The first step in understanding the lime making process is to realize that the composition of marble is the same as limestone, which is calcium carbonate. Lime is nothing more than calcium oxide. To change calcium carbonate into lime, one must heat the rock enough to chemically break down the ore and drive off carbon dioxide gas. This process is called lime burning and is done in a special furnace called a kiln. The temperature at which the ore breaks down varies from 1,648 degrees Fahrenheit to 1,022 degrees Fahrenheit, depending upon the amount of magnesium contained in the marble.

The typical lime kiln had a pair of fireboxes near its base. Wood was used as fuel and was burned in these fireboxes, and the draft drew the heat and smoke up through the kiln, baking the ore.

In 1902, J. Henry Roraback, along with several other men, formed the New England Lime Company by purchasing all of the competing lime companies in the entire western lime belt, from Redding, Connecticut, to North Pownal, Vermont. Most of these kilns were immediately closed, leaving only a select few in operation.

The U.S. Government purchased the New England Lime Company Canaan facility in 1942, and placed it under the control of the Atomic Energy Commission. The making of lime ceased, and a new plant was built on site of the Daisy Hill kiln to produce magnesium metal from the marble. The new company was called NELCO. Magnesium for the first atomic bomb came from the NELCO plant in Canaan.

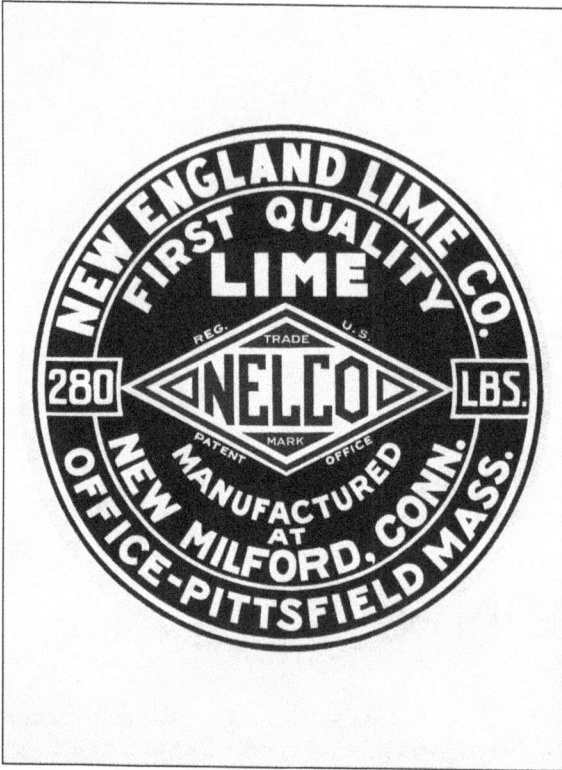

Most of the lime produced in Connecticut was shipped in wooden barrels. This illustration is of a label that would have been glued to the end of a barrel of lime manufactured at the New England Lime Company's New Milford quarry. Other labels were used for different types of lime. (Courtesy of John A. Pawloski.)

Wildman's Kiln in Brookfield was built prior to 1835, and is known locally as the Northrop Kiln. When the burned lime was ready, it was raked into the wagon and then dumped on the cement floor where it was allowed to cool. The large wooden mallet was used to break up the larger lumps before the lime was shoveled into the barrels. This photograph was taken just before the kiln closed in 1910. (Courtesy of Robin Stack.)

106

In 1893, Charles E. Griffin constructed a lime quarrying and burning operation in the Boardman District of New Milford. The Griffin Quarry became one of the largest producers of lime in Connecticut. This photograph, taken around 1900, shows mules being used to tram the marble in rail cars. (Courtesy of John A. Pawloski, photograph by Clarence Evans.)

Charles E. Griffin's initial Boardman complex consisted of five kilns surrounded by wooden buildings. The kilns can be seen behind the numbered roof peaks. Daily wagon loads of wood were delivered to fuel the kiln fires. The large building is the warehouse. This photograph was taken around 1900. (Courtesy of John A. Pawloski, photograph by Clarence Evans.)

107

Seen here are the ruins of Charles E. Griffin's Boardman lime operation after a fire in 1902 destroyed all of the buildings. The lime kilns themselves are the cylindrical structures seen in the background. In that same year the New England Lime Company purchased the operation. (Courtesy of the New Milford Historical Society.)

The New England Lime Company rebuilt the Boardman kilns, only this time they used stone masonry, and they also added three more kilns for increased production. Eventually three quarries were mined on the property for the marble. They continued to produce lime at the Boardman plant until 1915. (Courtesy of the New Milford Historical Society.)

This photograph of coopers assembling wooden barrels was taken prior to the 1902 fire that devastated the Boardman lime operation. The barrels were made in Tennessee and shipped unassembled to the Boardman plant, where they were put together by Griffin's team of coopers. (Courtesy of the New Milford Historical Society.)

Charles E. Griffin, and later the New England Lime Company, operated a community for their workers. The village consisted of worker housing, a school, and a company store. Today all that remains are the quarries and a small brick building. The quarry is still being operated by the Advance Stone Company, and the rock is crushed for aggregate. (Courtesy of the New Milford Historical Society.)

The center of Connecticut's lime burning industry was undoubtedly the Falls Village-Canaan area. Dozens of small quarries and nearly 40 kilns were in use in the last 150 years. This is an early 1900s view of the New England Lime Company quarry on Lower Road in Canaan. (Courtesy of Specialty Minerals.)

This 1905 photograph is of the Allyndale Quarry in East Canaan. The quarry men are drilling holes by hand with hand steels and sledge hammers. The marble facing for the state capitol building was taken from the Allyndale Quarry. (Courtesy of the Falls Village-Canaan Historical Society.)

This 1905 view is of quarry men hand drilling the marble at the Allyndale Quarry in East Canaan. The blasted rock was further broken up using sledge hammers, and then mule-drawn wagons hauled the blasted stone to the kilns. (Courtesy of the Falls Village-Canaan Historical Society.)

This steam powered shovel was still being used by NELCO as late as 1955 in their quarry on Lower Road in Canaan. (Courtesy of Specialty Minerals.)

Lime Quarry, Canaan, Conn.

A postcard 1915 view of a Canaan lime quarry shows that small gauge rail cars were loaded with the blasted rock and trammed to the area of the quarry beneath the derrick. The derrick then lifted the loaded body of the car to the surface, where the ore was dumped into the stockpile behind the derrick and the body returned to the quarry pit. (Courtesy of John A. Pawloski.)

In 1964, NELCO sold the Canaan operation to the Pfizer Minerals Company, who stopped producing magnesium. Pfizer sold its ground marble to industries who used it in refining steel, the coating on chewing gum, cultured marble, medicine, and as a filler in floor tiles and ceiling tiles. In 1992, Pfizer sold its mineral division to its employees and it was renamed Specialty Minerals. This is a 1975 photograph of their quarry in Canaan. (Courtesy of Specialty Minerals.)

112

This is a 1960s photograph of the ore train used by the U.S. Gypsum Corporation when they operated a quarry just north of Falls Village. This quarry was first worked by the American Marble and Lime Company in the early 1860s, who sold it to the New England Lime Company in 1902. (Courtesy of the Falls Village-Canaan Historical Society.)

This is the Sharon Valley lime kiln, as seen in 1933. The kiln was unusual in that it was square in shape, more like an iron furnace. The kiln was built sometime in the 1800s, and was restored in 2004. (Courtesy of Frederick Chesson, photograph by Charles R. Harte.)

In 1920, when this photograph was taken, the Redding Lime Company operated two kilns near their quarry in West Redding. The loading ramps can be seen at the tops of the circular kilns, where all lime kilns in Connecticut were loaded. (Courtesy of John A. Pawloski.)

This is the Connecticut Lime Company in East Canaan in 1913. The tower supported a cable tramway that brought bucket loads of marble to the kiln, where it was dumped into the top of the kiln. (Courtesy of John A. Pawloski.)

Canfield Co. Lime Plant, East Canaan, Conn.

This postcard view of the Canfield Lime Company located in East Canaan is postmarked 1910. The kilns can be seen just behind the white warehouse. (Courtesy of John A. Pawloski.)

Lime Kiln and the Green Pond   Canaan, Conn.

This unidentified postcard of a lime kiln operation lists Canaan as its location. Three of the kilns are being burned. (Courtesy of John A. Pawloski.)

New England Lime Co.'s Kiln.   CANAAN, Conn.

One of the New England Lime Company's Canaan operations can be seen in this undated postcard view. The marble was hauled by wagon and dumped into the top of the kiln at this location. (Courtesy of John A. Pawloski.)

The ruins of a lime kiln operation are all that remains of a major Connecticut mining industry. The last Connecticut lime kiln, in Canaan, was shut down in 1942. This photograph was taken in 1943 in East Canaan. (Courtesy of Frederick Chesson, photograph by Charles R. Harte.)

The Conklin Lime Company and quarry are located on Sand Road in Falls Village. The company was a family run business founded by Charles Conklin and George Jastram in 1938 for the production of ground agricultural limestone. (Courtesy of the Conklin Lime Company.)

Originally the Conklin Lime Company produced agricultural lime and had a fleet of spreader trucks to service the farmers. Today they have diversified into producing aggregate and landscaping stone as well. (Courtesy of the Conklin Lime Company.)

At the junction of Route 67 and Dillon Road in Woodbridge are the ruins of a double rectangular lime kiln built in the 1800s. The quarry, which is just above the kiln, produced a poor quality ore, and the operation was a failure. This photograph was taken in 1933. (Courtesy of Frederick Chesson, photograph by Charles R. Harte.)

This illustration is an unissued specimen stock certificate of the New England Lime Company, founded in 1902. (Courtesy of John A. Pawloski.)

This is the interior of the New England Lime Company kiln shed on Daisy Hill Road in Canaan. This c. 1920 photograph shows workers (left) standing near piles of improperly burned ore. This ore was then fed back into the kiln to complete the process. The large round structure is the base of one of the kilns. (Courtesy of Specialty Minerals.)

A photograph of a quarry blast is captured on film shortly after detonation. This *c.* 1942 photograph was taken at the New England Lime Company's quarry on Lower Road in Canaan. (Courtesy of Specialty Minerals.)

This photograph was taken seconds after the previous photograph at the quarry on Lower Road in Canaan. (Courtesy of Specialty Minerals.)

Clareace Beverly is operating a St. Regis packer (bagging machine) at the Daisy Hill plant of the Pfizer Minerals Company in Canaan. (Courtesy of the Falls Village-Canaan Historical Society.)

In 1942, the New England Lime Company was sold to the U.S. Government. The Daisy Hill facility was rebuilt for the production of magnesium metal extracted from the marble. The new company was called NELCO and was under the control of the Atomic Energy Commission. The magnesium from this plant went into the making the first atomic bomb. (Courtesy of Specialty Minerals.)

This is one of the bagging operations, around 1955, at the NELCO magnesium plant on Daisy Hill Road in Canaan. (Courtesy of Specialty Minerals.)

This 1944 photograph shows the rotary furnaces used in smelting magnesium from the marble at the NELCO plant on Daisy Hill Road in Canaan. The process requires 12 tons of dolomitic marble mixed with one ton of ferrosilicon to produce one ton of magnesium metal. The NELCO plant in Canaan produced an average of 12 tons of magnesium per day. (Courtesy of Specialty Minerals.)

The ore mixture was placed at one end of the furnace and heated to 2,100 degrees Fahrenheit and baked for 12 hours. The magnesium was vaporized during the heating process, and was crystallized as a pure metal at the other end of the furnace that was cooled. Magnesium crystals can be seen inside the cylinders. This photograph was taken at the NELCO plant in Canaan around 1944. (Courtesy of Specialty Minerals.)

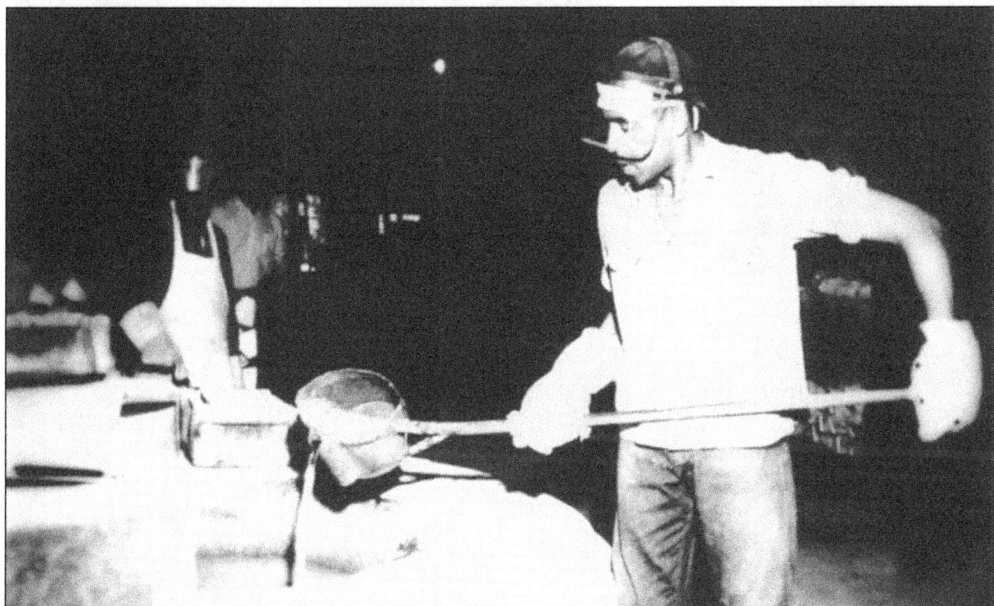

The magnesium crystals were then melted in small furnaces as seen in this photograph. Since magnesium will burn with an intense white flame in the presence of air, sulfur was sprinkled on the surface to lessen the danger of fire. The molten magnesium was then ladled out and poured into ingots. (Courtesy of Specialty Minerals.)

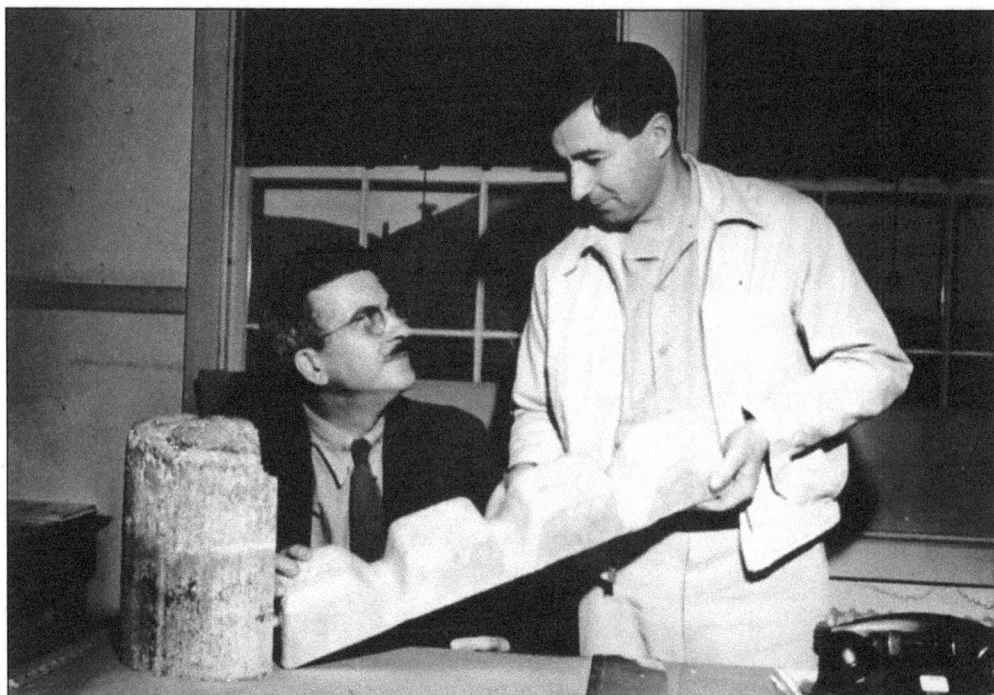

A cylinder of magnesium crystals and an ingot of the metal are seen in this 1955 NELCO photograph. In 1964, NELCO stopped producing magnesium. (Courtesy of Specialty Minerals.)

NELCO had its own analytical laboratory for determining the quality of the ore and other materials used in the manufacture of magnesium and calcium metal, which they also produced. This photograph was taken in 1955. (Courtesy of Specialty Minerals.)

Eight

BIRTH OF THE WORLDS AGGREGATE INDUSTRY

The crushed stone industry, also called aggregate, presently one of the most important mining industries in the United States, is just what its name implies—rock broken up into smaller pieces. In Connecticut, it has become the largest money producer of any mining industry in the state.

The earlier uses of crushed stone were primarily as a road fill and railroad ballast. The mid-1800s saw an increase in the construction of railroads, and most of the wagon roads were of dirt or mud depending upon the season. By adding a surface of crushed stone, these roads became less muddy and better suited for travel by horse and wagon.

In the early part of the 19th century, rock had to be broken manually. The industry became mechanized when a Connecticut inventor, Eli Whitney Blake, developed the first steam powered "jaw crusher" in 1858. A jaw crusher consists of two thick very heavy iron plates, one stationary and the other moving only a fraction of an inch towards the fixed plate and then back, thus repeating the cycle. With this large mechanical advantage developed by a heavy spinning flywheel, the rocks dropped between the two plates are crushed under the pressure.

Eli Whitney Blake's crusher was used in a small quarry in the West Rocks section of New Haven up to the 1880s.

While any rock can be used to make aggregate, the most desired are the hard durable rocks from the lava flows that formed during the Triassic/Jurassic periods in the Central Connecticut Valley and in the Woodbury area. These two types of rock, diabase and basalt, are collectively termed "traprock." The name traprock comes from the German word *treppen* meaning "steps," since the quarry walls had the appearance of steps.

Most Connecticut aggregate quarries were started by a blast into the side of a hill, and are worked from the top of the cliff down to the quarry floor in a bench method.

The large traprock quarry presently owned by the Tilcon Corporation at Totoket Mountain in Branford began around 1900 by Louis Fisk. In 1914, the Hayden and Stone Company merged with Fisk. A steam powered shovel is seen in this 1917 photograph, loading quarry cars with the blasted stone destined for the crusher. (Courtesy of the Tilcon Corporation.)

This photograph shows a steam traction engine powering a crusher, and the crushed stone which is produced is then conveyed to the top of the storage bins, as seen in this early-1900s photograph. (Courtesy of the Tilcon Corporation.)

In 1935, Hayden, Stone, and Fisk purchased the Connecticut Quarries Company and formed the New Haven Traprock Company. In this 1922 view, dump trucks are being loaded from the storage bins at the Totoket Quarry. (Courtesy of the Tilcon Corporation.)

In 1903, Louis Fisk constructed a three mile railroad connecting the Totoket Quarry to his barge loading dock at Pine Orchard on Long Island Sound in Branford. Today the Totoket Quarry is owned by Tilcon Connecticut, who still ships the aggregate by rail to the loading docks. This photograph of the Pine Orchard Loading docks was taken in 1912. (Courtesy of the Tilcon Corporation.)

Visit us at
arcadiapublishing.com